College of the
Holy Names

Library

Oakland - - California

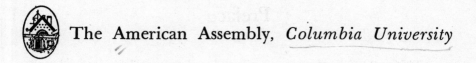

The American Assembly, *Columbia University*

THE POPULATION DILEMMA

Prentice-Hall, Inc., *Englewood Cliffs, N.J.*

A SPECTRUM BOOK

Preface

This collection of papers, written for the general reader under the supervision of Philip M. Hauser, University of Chicago, also comprised the background reading for the Twenty-third American Assembly at Arden House, Harriman (N.Y.) Campus of Columbia University, May 2-5, 1963. For three days participants in the Assembly discussed the facts and issues raised in the chapters which follow, and in plenary session on the fourth day reviewed the final report of findings and recommendations for national policy which begins on page 178.

The opinions expressed in these essays are not necessarily endorsed by The American Assembly, which takes no official stand on the subjects it presents for public deliberation. Neither do they represent the views of The Ford Foundation, The Population Council, Cordelia Scaife May, or Laurel Foundation, who generously supported the entire program.

Henry M. Wriston
Chairman
The American Assembly

Fifth printing ...... April, 1965

Table of Contents

Philip M. Hauser

1

Introduction and Overview

Our ever-shrinking, more complex and interdependent world is
increasingly confronted with global problems. Among those recognized
and dealt with historically are epidemics and contagious diseases; nar-
cotic and white slave traffic; postal, telegraphic and radio communication;
weather forecasting; and international air transport. New global problems
have emerged in the postwar world such as fallout and the exploration
and use of outer space. Another global problem of long making is becoming ever more acute and threatens to assume crisis proportions in the
coming generation. It is the problem posed by accelerating population
growth.

Certainly more attention is being devoted to population problems
today, nationally and internationally, than at any time since Malthus.
On the world scene a number of governments as a matter of policy are
striving to dampen rates of population increase by means of fertility control. These governments include Japan, India, Pakistan, Korea, Singapore, the United Arab Republic, Turkey, Tunisia, and with reversals
of policy, Mainland China. For this explicit formulation of the need to
control population growth is the product of three centuries of accelerating
world population increase unprecedented in scale—the "demographic
revolution." It is significant that on December 18, 1962, in the General

PHILIP M. HAUSER *is Chairman of the Department of Sociology, and Director of
the Population Research and Training Center at the University of Chicago. He
has combined an academic career with various United States Government and
international agency assignments, having served as Acting Director and Deputy
Director of the United States Bureau of the Census; United States Representative on the Population Commission of the United Nations; United Nations Statistical Advisor to Burma and to Thailand; and General Rapporteur of UN/
UNESCO Seminars on Urbanization in Asia and in Latin America. He is a Past
President of the American Statistical Association and of the Population Association of America; and Past Vice President of the American Sociological Association and of the American Association for the Advancement of Science. His
publications include* Population Perspectives, *1960 and* The Study of Population
(with O. D. Duncan), 1959.

1

Assembly of the United Nations, sixty-nine nations voted for and carried a resolution recognizing the relationship between population growth and economic development and requesting the United Nations to take certain steps designed to provide assistance on population problems. The nations which have made it a matter of policy to control their population growth may well be in the vanguard of a world-wide movement to face up to the implications of the demographic evolution.

On the national scene there is also ample evidence of the mounting interest in population growth and its consequences. There has been widespread public discussion of population problems and the pros and cons of birth control. Moreover, the federal government in recent years has taken cognizance of the relationship between population and economic development and the State Department has issued a "Statement of United States Policy." This statement expresses the concern of the United States about its own and world population trends, states that each nation must determine its own population policy, applauds the efforts of the United Nations and its affiliated agencies in this field, and offers to help other nations upon request "to find potential sources of information and assistance on ways and means of dealing with population problems."

This volume has been prepared as an aid to The American Assembly discussions. It sets forth the key population facts, the major problems being generated by accelerating growth, the basic policy issues, and the more important policy and action alternatives. The materials presented in the following chapters are thus designed to provide the reader with a sound basis for participating in the decisions on population matters that this democratic nation must make in the coming years.

An overview of world population growth, retrospectively and prospectively, is provided in Chapter 2 by Dr. Dorn. Despite the deficiencies in historical data, the fact that a remarkable acceleration in the rate of world population growth has occurred, especially in the past three centuries, is indisputable. Also indisputable is the explanation of this demographic revolution—man's increasing mastery over nature in effecting remarkable declines in mortality. Even though the major gains in longevity for most of the modern era, and especially before World War II, were restricted to a relatively small proportion of the world's peoples —those enjoying "Western civilization"—the explosive increase of Western populations together with the slower increase of the rest of the world's population produced amazing acceleration in total world growth.

Since the Second World War, the death rates in the non-western world have decreased sharply without the corresponding increases in productivity that occurred when western death rates declined over a longer period. Never before in the history of man have increasing numbers of persons been able to keep alive without increases in levels of living.

Given the new post-World War II situation, what is the prospect? In the long run the answer is quite clear. In less than a century and a half as Dr. Dorn reports, the highest estimate of the population-carrying capacity of the globe ever made by a competent scholar under extreme assumptions would be reached; and in about seven centuries there would be one person for every square foot of land surface on the globe. Such projections illustrating the effects of compound interest do not, of course, predict what future world population will be. But they do permit a highly significant and incontestible conclusion: the present rate of world population growth cannot possibly persist for very long into the future. In the long run, space is the limiting factor to population increase.

In the short run, the prospect is not quite so clear. For present and prospective rates of population increase have more indeterminate consequences affecting the economic, social, and political climates of individual nations as well as that of the world as a whole. The most significant consequence of rapid population growth in the contemporary world, however, is to be found in the relation of rapid population increase and its demographic accompaniments to economic development. In the short run the crucial effect of accelerating population growth, therefore, is to be found in the underdeveloped areas of the world. Population growth in the underdeveloped areas is Dr. Taeuber's subject in Chapter 3.

Continuation of present trends would, as Dr. Taeuber indicates, result in an increase of sixty five per cent in the population of the underdeveloped areas between 1950 and 1975 and a doubling of population in these areas in the last quarter of this century. Thus, the underdeveloped areas alone stand to experience a population increase in the second half of this century considerably greater than that achieved by all mankind in all of the millenia of his existence up to the current year! Since the "developed" areas would during the second half of this century increase by some 600 million persons—less than one-sixth of the increase in underdeveloped areas—the proportion of total world population in present underdeveloped areas would increase from two-thirds in 1950 to about four-fifths by 2000.

The populations of the underdeveloped areas are experiencing a "revolution of rising expectations"—to use Assistant Secretary of State Harlan Cleveland's felicitous phrase—against which their efforts to achieve higher levels of living seem frustratingly slow. The result is increasingly manifest. Political instability, subversion, revolution—all are associated with frustration and serve usually further to retard advance.

The way in which population growth and its demographic accompaniments tend to obstruct efforts to raise levels of living is comprehensively treated by Dr. Coale. He clearly traces the impact of population factors on per capita income and on productive employment of the labor force. He shows how a decline in the birth rate operates to increase per capita income, in the short run, by dampening the rate of population increase and reducing the burden of child dependency without major effect on the size of the labor force; and, in the longer run, by reduction in the growth rate of the labor force and lower population density. Reduced birth rates could increase income per consumer by over 40 per cent in thirty years, by 86 per cent in fifty years and more than 100 per cent in sixty years. "After one hundred and fifty years the low fertility population," concludes Coale, "would have an income per consumer six times as high as the faster growing population with unchanged fertility."

The chapters by Dr. Taeuber and Dr. Coale, within the framework of the world picture set forth by Dr. Dorn, clarify the crucial implications of contemporary rates of population increase for the underdeveloped areas and for the world as a whole. In doing this they also make it evident that the United States has a huge stake in both developments. For the citizenry of the United States there is no way to evade either the long-run implications of accelerating world population growth or the short-run consequences of events in the underdeveloped areas.

The fact that the population problem is an increasingly serious one in the United States itself is documented by Dr. Bogue in Chapter 5. Dr. Bogue points to both the short-run costs of our accelerated population increase and its long-run implications. The postwar rise in the birth rate of the United States which has produced a natural increase of over 1.6 per cent per annum, if sustained, would within a century produce a population of a billion Americans. He summarizes that this "would be roughly equivalent to moving all of the population of Europe, Latin America, and Africa into the territory of the fifty states." Even a return to our depression rate of natural increase, during the 1930's, a rate about half that of the present, would by 2065 produce a population of over 416 million persons. Such projected growth obviously has profound implications for the future style and level of living in the United States.

In the long run our present rate of population growth would exhaust all available space and, therefore, it cannot possibly be continued. But the problem is not only long run. As Dr. Bogue points out, although the effects of the baby boom are not all deleterious, we have already paid a high price for it and the price will continue to mount.

Among the more significant implications of accelerating population growth is that concerning its effect on the relation between population and resources—or the "man-land" ratio. The salient facts about resources in the United States and in the world are summarized in Chapter 6 by Dr. Fisher and Mr. Potter. Their answer to the question "Are resources becoming scarcer?" should, on the one hand, quiet the cries of alarmists who foresee early mass starvation and the imminent exhaustion of critical materials. On the other hand, they give reason for further reflection to the optimists who are convinced that man's ingenuity can resolve all the problems which may be precipitated by the increasing pressure of population on land and other resources.

Fisher and Potter provide the basic data for a realistic appraisal of the political significance of accelerating population growth. The world political problem posed is not one arising from any immediate threat of mass starvation or lowered living levels. It is, rather, that arising from the inability of the mass populations in the less developed areas to achieve significant increases in their levels of living consistent with their aspirations as generated by the "revolution of rising expectations." It is the continued frustration and poverty of the mass populations of the under-developed nations, to which rapid population growth contributes, that portends continued political instability and unrest. In the bipolar world rent by the Cold War, explosive population growth may thus become a major factor in determining whether the mass populations of the under-developed nations, still neutral or uncommitted, swing to the Free or Communist way of life.

What is to be done to control runaway population growth? There are only two ways to dampen world population increase. One is to in-crease the death rate and the other is to decrease the birth rate. There are no nations or cultures in the world prepared to accept an increase in mortality as a way of controlling population growth. In consequence, only the control of fertility remains as a way to check population increase. Fertility control and problems incident to it constitute the subject of Chapter 7 by Drs. Notestein, Kirk and Segal.

In view of the demographic prospects of the developing countries Dr. Notestein and his colleagues conclude that it is imperative that an effort be made by governmental as well as private means to effect reduc-tions in fertility. Although governmental programs to promote birth con-trol have not been operating long enough yet to prove their effectiveness, some success stories are already at hand, as for example in India and Ceylon. The evidences of success to date together with the prospect for improvement in methods of preventing conception lead the authors to moderate optimism about the outlook for regulating fertility.

Dr. Lorimer concludes this volume in his consideration of "issues of population policy." Recognizing that "questions of policy relative to population trends are, in large part, regional and specific . . . ," Lorimer nevertheless appropriately holds that "the development of American policies . . . must . . . be framed in a world context." Objective analy-sis is beset with obstacles of cultural and personal preconceptions—in-cluding the Neo-Malthusian and Marxist postures and the positions of diverse religious groups. Nonetheless it is necessary to face the issues and take the appropriate policy decisions.

Special policy issues include those arising from differential rates of natural increase in the U. S. by region, race and socio-economic status; from the redistribution of our population from rural to urban and metropolitan areas, and from the South to the North and West. Dr. Lorimer emphasizes the need to recognize "the nation is an interacting demographic unit." There is need also to face policy issues with respect to immigration; and to a number of social problems affected by population changes such as unemployment, school "dropouts," marginal workers and Aid to Dependent Children. Policy problems are also posed by our increasing numbers of older persons. In his presentation of issues of population policy Dr. Lorimer, on the one hand, touches on problems which must be faced by reason of past demographic history and, on the other, on problems that will arise in the future.

We are forced to live with and in some manner to deal with the population problems that we have inherited from the past. For example, under the pressures generated by our postwar resurgence in population growth, we have expanded our elementary school plant, and we are faced with doing the same during this decade with our secondary school and college plants. But despite our efforts, we are experiencing depreciation in the quality of our education. As our postwar babies reach labor force age during the sixties, we shall pay a high price in striving to provide jobs or support of some kind for our tidal wave of new workers. We seem to deal with the consequences of accelerated population growth only as they become acute problems that cannot be evaded.

It is easier to ignore the tasks that aim at preventing the population problems of the future. In consequence, we are expending huge resources for treating the deleterious consequences of past rapid population growth while, in the main, we continue to do little or nothing about the present excessive growth which will produce even more acute problems in the future. For example, as a nation we are just beginning to consider whether we should assist the underprivileged who desire such assistance to control their fertility—both within the United States itself and abroad.

In this situation lies the dilemma which gives this volume its title—the choice of unsatisfactory alternatives. It is to be found in the necessity to choose between continued indifference to the implications for the future of present population growth and the acceptance of the consequences of such indifference. To formulate appropriate population policy and take necessary action requires changes in established attitudes and behavior which meet with resistance—more from some quarters than from others. But to take the easy way out at the present time is to compound the difficulties of the future. To avoid the ounce of prevention in the present will, in the future, require many pounds of cure.

It is undoubtedly a fact that the vast majority of the people of the world, including a large proportion of the people in the United States, do not yet recognize this dilemma. It is the major purpose of this volume to call attention to it, to clarify the issues involved, and to press the point that to continue to ignore the population problem is, in effect, to choose one of the horns of the dilemma—the more costly and dangerous one.

Harold F. Dorn

2

World Population Growth

More than one million identified species of animals and plants inhabit the earth. Of these, only man can in part control and modify his environment. Because of this ability, he now dominates the earth to an extent probably never before approached by any other species. This dominance is very recent and has given rise to conditions to which man still is far from well adjusted.

The evolutionary process has endowed all species of plants and animals with a reproductive potential which, if unrestrained, would overpopulate the earth within a few generations. This reproductive potential has been and still is controlled by disease, limitation of the food supply, and interspecies competition in the struggle for existence. No organism has ever been able to free itself from the biological regulators of growth in number. Man is no exception to this principle.

NATURAL CHECKS ON GROWTH

Throughout the centuries of his existence man undoubtedly has had a birth rate which, if unchecked, long ago would have led to standing room only in the world. Until very recently, this excessive fertility has

HAROLD F. DORN *is Chief of the Biometrics Research Branch of the National Heart Institute, U. S. Public Health Service. He has represented the United States at important international conferences on population and public health matters. He has played a prominent role in United States population statistics and research in various capacities including service on the Technical Advisory Committee for the 1950 Population Census and on the United States National Committee on Vital and Health Statistics. Dr. Dorn is a Past President of the Population Association of America; and a Fellow of the American Public Health Association, the American Association for the Advancement of Science, and the American Statistical Association.*

been controlled, just as for all other species, by an almost equally high mortality. During this century one of the most significant developments for the future of mankind has been his increasing ability to control two of the three natural regulators of population increase—disease and famine.

It is difficult to realize today how effectively disease and famine have acted as a check upon the increase of population during the centuries of man's existence, and how recently the effectiveness of these checks has been curbed. The last great famine of Western Europe occurred in Ireland about 115 years ago. A severe shortage of food lasted for nearly six years. In spite of assistance from other countries, one out of every eight persons alive at the beginning of the famine in 1846 died during the following five years.

In the present century, between twenty-five and thirty million deaths in excess of those that normally would have been expected are estimated to have taken place in the Soviet Union in the twelve-year period, 1914-1926, as a result of war, famine, and disease. Severe shortages of food still occur in local areas as evidenced by those in India in 1943 and 1951, in Brazil in 1961, and possibly in China during recent years. From the global point of view, however, the famines of the present century have been a minor check upon world population increase in comparison to those of the past.

Disease historically has waged a close struggle with famine for first place as a regulator of population increase. At least one-fourth of the population is thought to have died when the Black Death swept through Europe around the middle of the fourteenth century. Three hundred years later, the Great Plague of 1664-1665 killed one-sixth of the population of London.

In 1832, 1849, and 1854 epidemics of cholera raised the death rate in New York City to more than forty-five per 1,000 per year. It was not until the 1870's that the crude death in New York City permanently dropped below thirty per 1,000.

THE DEMOGRAPHIC REVOLUTION

Around 1700, the expectation of life at birth of the white population of North America and of Western Europe was about thirty-three years and probably had increased very little during the preceding three or four centuries. In 1950, the expectation of life at birth of the white population of the United States was sixty-nine years, an increase of more than 100 per cent. Nearly all populations of Western and Central Europe participated in this gain in longevity.

Four factors were primarily responsible for this dramatic increase in longevity: (a) the opening up of new continents, which provided additional sources of food, precious metals, and raw materials as well as an outlet for an increasing population; (b) the expansion of commerce, which made possible the transportation of food and capital goods over long distances; (c) technological changes in agriculture, together with the development of modern industry; and (d) increased control of disease by means of improved housing, better food and water supplies, adoption of sanitary measures, the growth of knowledge of preventive medicine, and discoveries in pharmacology and chemotherapy, particularly antibiotics and insecticides.

These developments upset the near balance between fertility and mortality that had existed during the previous centuries. Following the drop in the death rate, the European population multiplied rapidly. There were about 100 to 120 million Europeans in 1650. Three centuries later, the number of persons of European stock had increased eight-fold, reaching a total of about 940 million.

The rapid increase in population that followed the lowering of mortality rates was checked by the development of an effective substitute restraint upon uncontrolled fertility, namely, contraception. By the late 1920's, fertility had fallen so low that many demographers believed the population of European origin might soon begin to decrease in number. Voluntary control of fertility had proved to be fully as effective a regulator of population growth as disease and famine.

This shift—from a relatively low rate of increase due to the restraining effect of a high death rate upon a high birth rate to a correspondingly low rate of increase due to the voluntary control of fertility which brought about a fall in the birth rate to the low level reached by the death rate—is known as the demographic revolution. Less than one-third of the world's population participated in this revolution.

At the beginning of this century the remaining two-thirds of the world's population—the people of Africa, Latin America, and Asia—had an estimated birth rate of forty or more per 1,000 per year and a death rate only slightly lower. Since then the scientific knowledge and technical skill that brought about the remarkable increase of longevity in North America, Europe, Australia, and New Zealand have become available to the remainder of the world's population. The result has been an absolute increase in number unparalleled during the recorded history of mankind.

Past growth

The number of persons living in the world today is known only approximately. Even less is known about the size of the world's population at various times in the past. Although records of occasional attempts to count the population living in selected areas of the world go back to the dawn of written history, regular censuses of population did not exist

TABLE I

Estimated population of the world and the number of years required for it to double

Year (A.D.)	Population (billions)	Number of years to double
1	0.25 (?)	1650 (?)
1650	0.50	200
1850	1.1	80
1930	2.0	45
1975	4.0	35
2010	8.0	?

in any country prior to 1800. Reliable population counts even today are regularly available for less than one-half of the population of the world.

The generally accepted estimates of the population of the world prior to 1900 are derived from fragmentary statistics supplemented by informed guesses. As one goes backward in time, the available statistics become increasingly more fragmentary and unreliable, so that the earliest estimates represent only informed guesses.

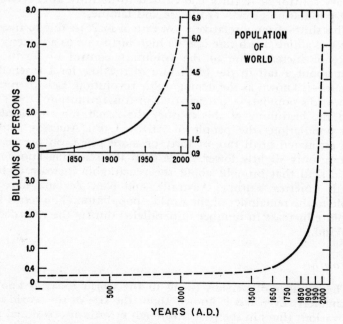

Figure 1. Estimated population of the world from 1 A.D. to 1960 A.D. and the projected population 2000 A.D.

Nevertheless, scholars have pieced together a consistent series of guesses and estimates of the growth of the world's population during the past two thousand years that appear plausible. The most generally accepted estimates are presented in Figure 1 and Table 1.

The length of time that the present subgroups of man have inhabited the earth is unknown. Most estimates range from 50,000 to 200,000 years, although some are even longer. Enough is known, however, to support the belief that many millennia were required for mankind to increase in number until he reached a global total of one-quarter of a billion persons. This occurred about 2,000 years ago.

Sixteen centuries passed before another quarter-billion persons were added to the world's population. The Pilgrims had landed at Plymouth Rock and had founded the Massachusetts Bay Colony at about the time the population of the world reached a total of half a billion.

In contrast to the hundreds of centuries that elapsed before the first half billion was reached, only two centuries were required for the second half billion. Shortly before the outbreak of the Civil War, it is estimated that one billion persons inhabited the earth. The addition of successive half billions of persons has required increasingly shorter periods of time. The sixth half billion, just added, required slightly more than ten years. At the present rate of growth only six or seven years will be required to add the eighth half billion. This change in population growth has taken place since the first settlers came to New England.

Increase in longevity

This acceleration in the rate of growth of the world's population has resulted from a rapid decline in mortality rates with a consequent sharp increase in the average expectation of life. Accurate statistics do not exist, but the expectation of life at birth in Greece, Rome, and Egypt during a period of perhaps 500 years around the beginning of the Christian Era probably did not exceed thirty years. Nineteen hundred years later, the populations of North America and Western Europe had added another fifteen to twenty years to their expectation of life, thus reaching a total of forty-five to fifty years. Today another twenty years has been added. The increase in expectation of life at birth for these peoples during the past half century has been as great or greater than that during the previous years.

By 1940, only a minority of the population of the world had experienced the spectacular increase in longevity just described. The longevity of the majority of persons was no greater than that of Western Europeans during the Middle Ages. During the past two decades, the possibility of achieving a twentieth-century death rate has been opened to the masses of the world who still had a medieval death rate. An indi-

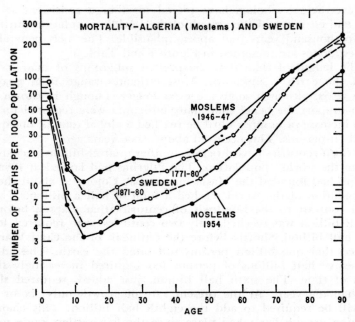

Figure 2. The decline in mortality in Sweden from 1771-80 to 1871-80 and for the Moslem population of Algeria, 1946-47 to 1954.

cation of what can be achieved by the application of existing knowledge concerning the control of disease is shown in Figure 2.

Spread of decline in mortality

In 1946-47, the death rate of the Moslem population of Algeria was higher than that of the population of Sweden more than a century and a half earlier, 1771-80. During the following eight years the decrease in the death rate in Algeria was greater than that in Sweden during the century from 1775 to 1875.

Corresponding precipitous declines in the death rate have occurred during the past twenty years in many countries of Asia and Latin America (Table 2). The death rate for most countries of Africa probably did not decline appreciably during this period, but population and vital statistics throughout most of this continent are too incomplete and unreliable to warrant a more precise statement. However, the data in Table 2 suggest that the death rate in those countries of Asia, Africa, and Latin America where eighteenth century mortality conditions still prevail can rapidly be lowered by a thorough utilization of existing knowledge of preventive medicine, sanitation, and nutrition.

TABLE 2

Changes in the crude death rate for selected countries 1940 to 1960

Country	Number of deaths per 1,000 population		
	1940	1950	1960
Mexico............................	23.2	16.2	11.4
Costa Rica........................	17.3	12.2	8.6
Chile.............................	21.6	15.0	11.9
Venezuela.........................	16.6	10.9	8.0
Ceylon............................	20.6	12.4	9.1
Malaya............................	20.1	15.9	9.5
Singapore.........................	20.9	12.0	6.3
Japan.............................	16.8	10.9	7.6

The worldwide reduction in mortality is the most significant demographic event during this century and symbolizes both the extent to which man can now control his environment and the rapidity with which this control has been achieved. This nullification of the effect of the historic governors of unrestrained fertility has resulted in a spurt in population increase that cannot long continue.

Implication of mortality decline

The increase in the rate of growth of the world's population shown in Table 1 is still continuing. It requires only very simple arithmetic to show that a continuation of the present rate of growth for even ten to twenty decades would result in a numerical increase in population that would make this globe resemble an anthill.

The four billion persons expected by 1975 would become thirty-two billion a century later; in another century and a quarter, by 2200, their descendants would number 500 billion. If uniformly distributed over the entire land surface of the earth, covering deserts, jungles, mountains, and the frozen arctic regions, the density of population would be slightly less than that of Washington, D. C. in 1960.

Numbers of this size stagger the imagination. We cannot conceive of how such a population could exist. It seems inevitable that man must consciously re-establish control over his reproductive potential and lower his birth rate to the level of his death rate before another century has elapsed. If he does not, he will lose his power to control his future and the former regulators of population increase will once again reign supreme.

The accelerating rate of increase in population growth has come about so unobtrusively that most persons, even though dimly aware of its existence, are unaware of its implications. There is a small group who are so disturbed by this indifference that they have attempted to arouse the public with sensational phrases such as "the population bomb" and "the population explosion."

These persons are considered alarmists by others who point out that similar warnings, such as "standing room only," have been issued periodically since Malthus about 200 years ago enunciated his famous principle that population tends to increase more rapidly than the food supply. This latter group points out that history has proved the alarmists to be wrong. The level of living and the health of most of the population of the world have continued to improve in spite of its increase in number, and there is no reason to believe that advances in science and technology will not make possible a slowly rising level of living for a growing world population for many years to come. Furthermore, the demographic history of persons of European stock indicates that the rate of population increase almost certainly will slow down as the level of education and living rises and as urbanization increases.

ESTIMATED MAXIMUM POPULATION

Several persons have attempted to dramatize the implications of the recent increase in population by estimating the maximum population that could be supported provided existing technological knowledge were fully utilized. The range of these estimates is very wide. One of the lowest, 2.8 billion, made in 1945, already has been surpassed. Several others, ranging from five to seven billion, almost certainly will be exceeded by the end of this century. The largest—that of fifty billion prepared by Harrison Brown—would be reached in less than a century and a half.

All of the estimates, except that of Harrison Brown, of the maximum world population that could be supported without a drastic lowering of the existing level of living already have been shown to be unduly pessimistic. This has been interpreted as demonstrating that mankind will be able to provide for its increase in number for the indefinite future. Although it seems almost inevitable that the population of the world, before many decades have passed, may reach a size that, based on present knowledge, can be supported only by a lowering of the present level of living, the debate concerning the magnitude of this size and the date at which it may be reached has detracted attention from another aspect of population growth that is of more immediate importance.

The world is not a unit

Estimates of the maximum population that could be supported are rather unrealistic and are primarily useful only as very crude guidelines. They have assumed that the earth's resources and technological knowledge are a single reservoir available to all. In reality this is untrue. The government of the United States attempts to restrict production of certain agricultural crops while simultaneously hundreds of thousands of persons in Africa and Asia are undernourished and inadequately clothed.

The world is not a single political unit. Knowledge, technical skill, and capital are concentrated in areas with the highest level of living, whereas the most rapid increase in population is taking place in areas where such skills and capital are scarce relative to need. Hence, the increase in production of industrial and agricultural commodities actually achieved during any period of time is considerably less than that theoretically possible.

Just as the world is not a single unit from the viewpoint of needs and the availability of resources, skills, and knowledge to meet these needs, so it also is not a single unit with respect to population increase. Because of existing political barriers, the growth of population will become a serious problem in specific countries long before it would be a world problem if there were no barriers to population redistribution. Except in a very general sense there is no *world* population problem, but there are population problems varying in nature and degree among the different nations of the world. No single solution is applicable to all.

The immediate problem

The most immediate problem is the imbalance between the rate of population growth and the knowledge, capital, and resources to provide for the resulting increase in population that exists throughout the world today. The events of the past few years have graphically demonstrated how the political and economic problems of a small and weak nation can directly affect the welfare of the largest and most powerful nations. The effects of population growth like disease and atomic fallout transcend national boundaries. Rather than speculate about the maximum population the world can support and the length of time before this number will be reached, it is more instructive to examine the demographic changes that are taking place in different regions of the world and to comment briefly on their implications.

Regional population growth

The present population of the world is unevenly distributed over the land surface of the earth (Figure 3). Two-thirds of the world's population lives on about seven per cent of the land area. The most densely populated areas are Eastern and South Central Asia, Europe, and Northeastern United States. This distribution represents an adjustment of population to natural resources that has been worked out over thousands of years.

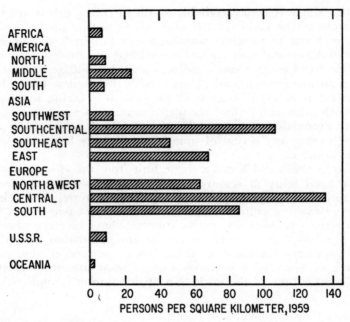

Figure 3. Number of persons per square kilometer in various regions of the world, 1960.

It also reflects the differing growth rates of the population of the separate regions during past centuries (Figure 4). The population of Europe and North America grew rapidly throughout the nineteenth century. During the twentieth century, first the population of Latin America and now that of many countries of Asia and Africa have begun to increase at a more rapid rate than those of Europe and North America. By 1960, the number of persons in Latin America exceeded the number in North America for the first time in more than a century. A continuation of present rates of growth for another forty years will result in a population in Latin America that is twice as large as that of North America.

Regional birth and death rates

The absolute level of fertility and mortality in different regions of the world is only approximately known. The United Nations estimates that only about thirty-three per cent of the world's deaths and forty-two per cent of the world's births are registered. The percentage registered varies widely throughout the world, ranging from about ten per cent in

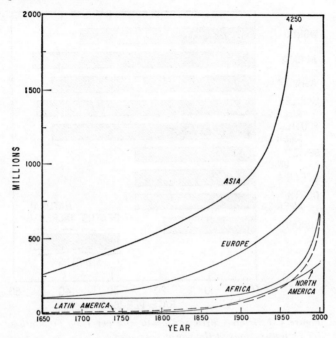

Figure 4. Estimated population of major regions of the world from 1650 to 1960 and the projected population in the year 2000.

tropical and Southern Africa and Eastern Asia to essentially complete registration in North America and Europe.

Using such data as are available, the statistical staff of the United Nations has prepared estimates of the birth and death rates in the different regions of the world that are believed to be a reasonably correct representation of the existing regional levels of fertility and mortality. The most recent estimates are shown in Figure 5.

The birth rate of most of the countries of Africa, Asia, Middle America and South America averages forty or more per 1,000 per year, little if any lower than it was 1,000 years ago. A few countries in these regions, such as Japan in Asia and the Union of South Africa in Africa, have birth rates less than one-half the regional average; hence some countries must have rates well above this average. In the rest of the world—Europe including the USSR, North America, and Oceania—the birth rate averages about twenty to twenty-five per 1,000 per year.

In contrast to the birth rates, the death rate for most of the countries of Africa, Asia, and Latin America, although still higher than that of the rest of the world—primarily persons of European stock—is rapidly

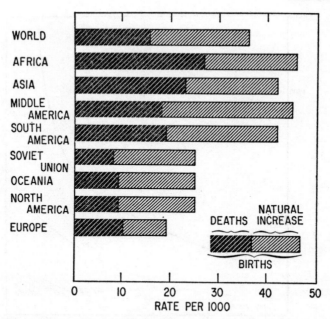

Figure 5. Estimated birth and death rate per 1,000 population for various regions of the world 1955-1959.

falling, with the result that the highest rates of natural increase are found in the regions with the highest birth rates, which are also the regions with the lowest levels of living. The most rapid rate of population growth at present is in Central and South America, where the population will double every twenty-six years if the present rate continues as all signs at present indicate.

Trend in the birth rate

It is the combination of a medieval birth rate with a twentieth-century death rate that is responsible for the current high rate of population increase. Not only is the birth rate high but, with a few exceptions, there is no indication that it will soon begin to fall. Because of the incompleteness of vital statistics in most of the countries that are believed to have the highest rates of population increase, it is impossible to do more than roughly estimate the trend. Data for a few selected countries in Latin America and Asia that have reasonably accurate vital statistics and for which the trend in fertility and mortality is believed to be similar to that for many other countries in the same regions are shown in Table 3. These are the same countries for which death rates are presented in Table 2.

TABLE 3

Changes in the crude birth rate for selected countries 1940 to 1960.

Country	Number of births per 1,000 population		
	1940	1950	1960
Mexico...........................	44.3	45.5	45.0
Costa Rica........................	44.6	45.9	42.9
Chile.............................	33.4	34.0	35.4
Venezuela........................	36.0	42.6	49.6
Ceylon...........................	35.8	39.7	37.0
Malaya...........................	40.7	42.3	37.7
Singapore.........................	45.0	45.4	38.7
Japan............................	29.4	28.2	17.2

Except for Japan, the birth rate for none of these countries has changed appreciably during the past two decades. In the meantime, as shown by the data in Table 2, the death rate dropped about fifty per cent. The experience of Japan illustrates that the rate of population growth may still remain almost unchanged even though the birth rate falls fairly rapidly, as long as the death rate falls even more rapidly. The birth rate in Japan decreased about forty per cent between 1940 and 1960, but the rate of natural increase decreased only one-half as much.

But Japan is not representative of most of the other countries in this group for which the crude rate of natural increase has risen. As a result, those countries with the highest rates of increase are experiencing an acceleration in their rates of growth. An illustration of what is happening in many of these countries is provided by Brazil. At the beginning of this century, in 1900, its population was estimated to be seventeen million. The census of 1950 reported 52 million, a three-fold increase in half a century. Ten years later, in 1960, 71 million persons were enumerated. At the current rate of increase, the population of Brazil will number between 235 and 240 million in the year 2000, or approximately fourteen times the number at the beginning of the century. Part of this astounding increase in number may be due to a more complete enumeration of the population during recent censuses than at the beginning of the century, but even a ten to twenty per cent underenumeration in 1900 would not appreciably alter the conclusions drawn from the official statistics.

Population and resources imbalance

The pattern of population growth just described enhances the existing imbalance between the distribution of the world's population and the distribution of wealth, available and utilized resources, and the use of nonhuman energy. One of the best indices of the ability of a country to provide a rising level of living for an increasing population is the amount of nonhuman energy it has available to devote to this purpose. The productivity of a modern industrial society is made possible only by an ever increasing use of nonhuman energy which enables one worker today to produce as much as several workers a generation ago.

Figure 6 shows the annual rate of population increase and the per capita consumption of energy for broad regions of the world. The people

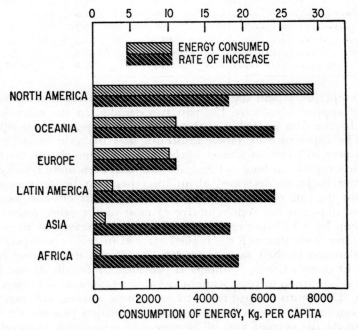

Figure 6. Number of kilograms of energy consumed per capita 1960 and the annual rate of population increase 1955-1959, by regions of the world.

of North America and Europe who make up twenty-eight per cent of the world's population use seventy-eight per cent of the nonhuman energy. In other words, one-fourth of the world's population consumes three-fourths of the energy. The rapid population increase in Asia, Africa, and Latin America acts as a brake on economic development since a large proportion of the relatively meager energy resources must be devoted to feeding, clothing, and educating the ever increasing number of babies.

ESTIMATES OF FUTURE POPULATION

What of the future? Is the present spurt in population growth a temporary phenomenon that will shortly cease with the birth rate falling to near the level of the death rate, or will it continue until the former biological regulators—war, disease, and famine—once again take control? Most demographers believe that the future population of individual nations, or of regions, or even of the entire world cannot be predicted for more than a few decades with more than a moderate degree of certainty. It is possible, however, to calculate the future population that would result from a continuation of present rates of growth or from some modification of these rates.

Such projections prepared by the United Nations are presented in Table 4. The actual population growth since these projections were pub-

TABLE 4

Estimated population of the world and its major regions, 1900, 1960, and 2000. (Millions)

Area	Estimated Population			Projected Population	Increase	
	1900	1950	1960	2000	1900 to 1950	1950 to 2000
World...................	1,550	2,518	2,995	6,907	968	4,389
Africa....................	120	209	254	663	89	454
North America............	81	168	199	326	87	158
Latin America.............	63	163	206	651	100	488
Asia......................	857	1,389	1,679	4,250	532	2,861
Europe inc. USSR..........	423	576	641	987	153	411
Oceania..................	6	13	17	30	7	17

lished five years ago indicates that even the highest projected values, those shown in Table 4, will be an underestimate of the population in the year 2000, less than forty years from now. The projected absolute increases in population during the second half of this century are expected to be two to five times larger than those during the first half. Numerical increases of this magnitude will create problems that may be beyond the ability of the nations concerned to solve.

The estimated increase in the population of Asia will be approximately equal to the total population of the world in 1958! The absolute increase in the population of Latin America during the last half of this century may equal the total increase in population of man during all the millennia from his origin until 1650, when the first colonists were settling New England.

Increases of this magnitude are almost incomprehensible and make us wonder whether they can take place. However, one-quarter of this period already has elapsed and population growth so far has slightly exceeded the high projections prepared by the United Nations. Furthermore, there is no evidence that the increase in the rate of growth shown by the data in Table 1 will soon cease. The world's population is estimated to be now growing about two per cent per year; at this rate it will double every thirty-five years. A continuation of this rate of growth for even ten or fifteen decades would result in an increase in population that would be several times the largest estimate of the maximum population that could be supported by present knowledge and technology.

It is the contemplation of these possibilities that has led many persons to think of the world's population problem as being mainly one of numbers and to concern themselves with the question of how many persons can be supported by the full use of existing knowledge and technology. This problem sometimes is rather narrowly conceived of as whether enough food can be produced to fill an ever increasing number of hungry mouths. Put in this simple way, the answer is obvious. Of course there will be sufficient food to support the increase in population; if there is not, population will not continue to increase. This is a biological law that no species has ever been able to evade.

The question of the size of the world's population is important, but concentration on this single aspect of the population problem diverts attention from one of more immediate importance, the effect of a rapid increase in numbers on the economic development and level of living in those countries of the world whose economy still is largely based upon human energy, a large share of which must be devoted to feeding, clothing, and educating the new generations at the expense of raising the existing low level of living.

There is no central granary from which the hungry can draw food as it is needed. Long before the population of the entire world reaches a size that could not be supported at current levels of living, the increase in population in individual nations will give rise to problems that will affect the welfare of the rest of the world. Let us turn our attention then to some of the effects and implications of the existing imbalance between population growth, land area, and natural resources. First, consider some demographic effects.

Demographic effects

A drop in the death rate, while the birth rate of a population remains unchanged, not only results in an increase in the rate of population growth but also produces an acceleration or increase in the rate of growth itself. This is demonstrated by the demographic history of recent decades. A decline in age specific mortality rates prior to the childbearing ages has the same demographic effect as an increase in the birth rate.

Another important effect of the decline in mortality rates often is overlooked, namely the increase in effective fertility. Under mortality conditions in the United States in 1950, ninety-seven out of every one hundred newborn white females would survive until age twenty, slightly past the beginning of the usual childbearing age, and ninety-one would survive to age fifty, the end of the childbearing period (Figure 7).

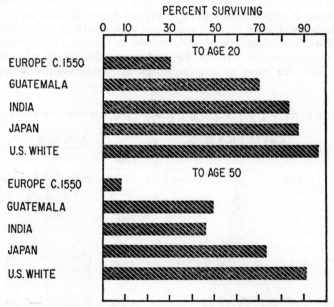

Figure 7. Percentage of newborn females who would survive to the end of the childbearing period according to mortality rates in Europe around 1500 and in selected countries around 1950.

In contrast, about seventy out of every one hundred newborn females in Guatemala would survive to age twenty and only forty-nine would survive to age fifty if subject to the death rates prevailing in that country in 1950. If the death rate in Guatemala should fall to the level of that in the United States in 1950, the number of newborn females out of each year's births who would survive to the beginning of the childbearing period would increase thirty-six per cent; the number surviving to the end of the childbearing period would increase eighty-five per cent. The birth rate would have to decrease more than forty per cent merely to prevent this increase in survivorship from resulting in an acceleration in the existing high rate of population growth.

With the exception of Japan, the birth rate in countries with high fertility has remained essentially unchanged. A drop of forty per cent in the birth rate of Japan between 1940 and 1960 only decreased the rate of natural increase from 1.3 to 1.0 per cent per annum. The experience of Japan, when viewed in the light of the decline in the death rate shown in Table 2, forecasts an almost inevitable acceleration in the rate of population increase for the two-thirds of the world's population that has not yet passed through the demographic revolution.

The rapid rate of natural increase of countries with a high birth rate produces a population with a relatively high proportion of children and adolescents (Figure 8). Forty-four per cent of the population of Costa Rica is less than fifteen years old, nearly twice the corresponding percentage, twenty-four, in Sweden. Percentages in the neighborhood of forty per cent exist for most of the countries of Africa, Latin America and Asia.

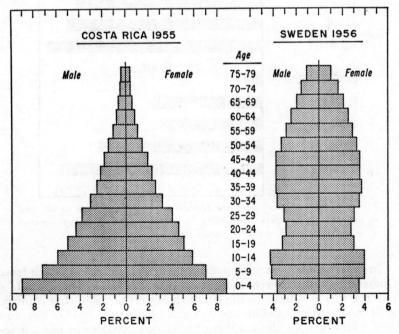

Figure 8. Percentage distribution by age of the population of Costa Rica in 1955 and of the population of Sweden in 1956.

This high proportion of young persons constitutes a large fertility potential for the next thirty years that can be counterbalanced only by a sharp decline in the birth rate. A large proportion of available labor and capital must be devoted to feeding, clothing, and educating them. Even though this is done at a relatively low level it causes a heavy drain upon the capital formation necessary to increase the productivity per worker and thus to improve the level of living of the entire population. The magnitude of this problem is illustrated by the five-year plan for India for 1961-66, which estimates that it will be necessary to provide educational facilities and teachers for twenty million additional children during this five-year period.

A continuation of the present pattern of population increase will alter the relative numerical standing of the major population groups of the world (Figure 9). During the past decade six out of every ten persons added to the world's population live in Asia; another two live in Latin America and Africa. It seems inevitable that the breaking up of the domination of the world by Northwest Europeans and their descendants, which already is well advanced, will continue, and that the center of power and influence will shift toward the demographic center of the world.

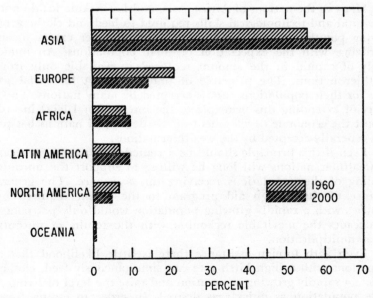

Figure 9. Percentage distribution of the world's population by regions, 1960 to 2000.

Economic and political implications

The demographic effects of the rapid rate of increase of countries
with a high fertility rate will produce widespread economic and political
repercussions. The present pattern of population increase enhances the
existing imbalance between the distribution of the world's population
and the distribution of wealth, available and utilized resources, and the
consumption of nonhuman energy. Probably for the first time in human
history there is a universal aspiration for a rapid improvement in the
standard of living and a rapidly growing impatience with conditions that
stand in the way of its attainment.

Millions of persons in Asia, Africa, and Latin America now are
aware of the standard of living enjoyed by Europeans and North Americans. They are demanding the opportunity to attain the same standard,
and they resist the idea that they must be permanently content with less.
As population continues to increase more rapidly than ability to satisfy
needs and desires, political unrest, perhaps leading to the violent over-
throw of existing governments, becomes almost inevitable. The tempta-
tion to adopt a dictatorial form of government in order to achieve more
quickly the desired rise in level of living may become irresistible for many
countries.

Many of the nations of Africa, Asia, and Latin America do not have
the capital and technological skills required to feed and clothe a rapidly
growing population and simultaneously to raise per capita income in
accordance with the expectation of their populations. An immediate
supply of capital in the amount required is available only from the
wealthier nations. The principle of public support for social welfare
plans for their populations is now accepted by many nations. The desir-
ability of extending this principle to the international level in order to
support the economic development of less developed nations has not yet
been generally accepted by the wealthier nations.

Even if this principle should be accepted, it is not as yet clear that
the wealthier nations will long be willing to support the uncontrolled
breeding of the populations receiving this assistance. The general acceptance of the foreign aid program to the extent required by the
countries with a rapidly growing population would only postpone for a
few decades the inevitable reckoning with the results of uncontrolled
human multiplication.

Even with foreign assistance there is little likelihood that all of
the nations with a high birth rate can simultaneously feed, clothe, and
educate a rapidly growing population and raise the level of living of the
entire population as quickly as desired. In order to escape from this
dilemma some of the larger nations may be tempted to try to seize the
relatively less crowded territory of more slowly growing neighbors. Recent

events have demonstrated that such acts may quickly involve nations far removed geographically from the scene of action and thus threaten the peace and welfare of the entire world.

The day of free migration has passed. International migration now is controlled by political considerations; for most of the population of the world, population pressure no longer can be even temporarily relieved by migration. Since more than one-half of the earth's land area is considered uninhabitable or undesirable, the continuation of the present rate of growth of the world's population for even a few decades will intensify the crowding of people on the most desirable land.

It is difficult to realize the implications of the arithmetic of the current growth of population. The number of persons in the world is so large that even a small rate of natural increase will result in an almost astronomical increment over a period of time of infinitesimal duration compared to the past history of the human race. As was pointed out above, continuation of the present rate of increase would result in a population of 500 billion persons in only twenty-four decades.

Past experience indicates that the future increase in population will tend to crowd into the territory considered most desirable by the existing population. Increasing density of population in huge urban centers must inevitably result in the loss of individual freedom irrespective of the kind of national government. The complexity of the economic and social structure of a large, densely populated metropolis necessitates many restrictions upon the freedom of action of the persons living there. As the population of such centers grows in size and density the extent of the restrictions upon individual freedom will inevitably increase.

Can man control his fertility?

The results of human reproduction no longer are solely the concern of the two persons immediately involved, nor of their families, nor even of the nation of which they are citizens. A stage has been reached in the demographic development of the human race when the rate of reproduction in any part of the globe may affect the health and welfare of the rest of the world's population. It is in this sense that there is a world population problem.

The future may witness a dramatic increase in man's ability to control his environment, to attain freedom from hunger, privation, and disease, and to explore outer space. The realization of this possibility depends on his ability to develop and quickly adopt cultural substitutes for the harsh but effective regulators of his high reproductive potential—disease and famine—that he so recently has learned to control. Man has unravelled many of the secrets of nature and has learned how to control or modify many natural phenomena, but he has not discovered how to evade the consequences of the biological law that no species can multiply without limit.

There are two ways to control a rapid increase in number—a high mortality or a low fertility. Alone, among the millions of biological organisms, man can choose which of these controls shall be used, but one of these must be. The choice cannot be avoided; the time for making a free choice will soon pass.

Irene B. Taeuber

3

Population Growth in
Underdeveloped Areas

Rapid population growth is a major fact of our era. Its association with poverty, malnutrition, illiteracy, and political instability are widely known. Projections of recent trends in growth to the end of the century yield a total of almost seven billion—a number few can comprehend. Continuing projections to the end of the twenty-first century yield a total of more than a hundred billion—a number still fewer can comprehend and none can believe.

Today rapid rates of population growth are leading to rapid increases in the numbers of the ill fed and the poorly housed. Must death rates then rise again to cut back man's numbers? None of earth's awakened peoples would admit this as a possibility. And indeed it is obvious to all that advancing science and technology will permit an adequate life for the people who now live on the earth or who may live on it at the century's end. What, then, is the problem?

The critical aspect of the many population problems of the contemporary world is that of timing. Rapid population growth would not be a major problem if it occurred along with rapid economic and social

IRENE B. TAEUBER *is Senior Research Demographer, Office of Population Re-search, Princeton University. She is a Past President of the Population Association of America, and currently a Vice President of the International Union for the Scientific Study of Population and a Fellow of the American Statistical Association. Her books include, as co-author,* The Future Population of Europe and the Soviet Union *(1943),* Public Health and Demography in the Far East *(1949), and* The Changing Population of the United States *(1958); as author,* General Censuses and Vital Statistics in the Americas *(1943),* The Population of Tanganyika *(1949), and* The Population of Japan *(1958).*

development. But if the major problem is the achievement of economic growth, population growth is a major hazard (See Chapter 4).

It would seem that the slowing of population growth would be a major aspect of development planning. If so, small families should rank along with nutrition, health, and education as individual and national goals. This may occur in the future, but it seldom occurs today.

GROWTH: PROCESS AND RECOGNITION

Fifteen years ago, few people realized that population growth would be a problem for countries planning economic and social development. Sufficient finance, education, and community development were believed to be enough to produce rising levels of living. Hence it was believed that efficient policy should be concerned with economic development, education, health and welfare rather than with population.

The population growth that was barred from governmental concern was not growth itself but the birth rate. The yearning for health and longer life was universal, and the arguments for public health were compelling. Scientific and technical advances made it possible to curb malaria and tuberculosis efficiently and cheaply. Other health problems yielded to modern approaches. Death rates were disassociated from low productivity, illiteracy, malnutrition and unsanitary living conditions. With lowered death rates and high birth rates, populations increased without changes in ways of living or means of earning a living.

Those who formerly saw no major problems of population growth in the future now saw soaring populations as the villains of all tales. Omens of demographic doom were heralded in press, radio, and television. "Explosion" was a common designation, while "explosive" was a common adjective.

The changing attitudes toward population growth are widespread. This is true in the developing nations themselves. That part of the changed climate of opinion that traces to educated elites is understandable. Censuses, vital statistics, and population research are still deficient if viewed by the standards of advanced nations, but there have been advances in recent years. There is increasing knowledge of the increasing rates of population growth. There is increasing realization of its implications for economic growth, human welfare, and political stability. Estimates of future populations are viewed with alarm. Neither the broad facts of the present nor the general outlines of the future can be denied.

The ordinary man feels the pressures of increasing numbers in his own family and village. Children become burdens when education and training are responsibilities of parents. Two or more surviving sons mean division of the land. Perhaps, too, the increasing numbers of children mean that some of them cannot attend school. Jobs may be poor and few in the villages, the towns, and the cities. The listing of difficulties could be continued. It is obvious that increasing populations produce pressures that are felt throughout a society in many aspects of life.

The most discouraging aspect of life in the underdeveloped areas is the seeming immutability of the problems of food and hunger. Today the populations of Asia, Africa, and Latin America are half again as large as those of the prewar period. Food production has increased by almost the same proportion. Over-all, per capita food production in 1961-62 was slightly less than that of the years prior to the Second World War. This is true for Eastern and Southern Asia, Northern Africa, and Latin America.

The trends are ironic indeed for a world dedicated to the advance of welfare. Populations increase least, food production most, in the developed countries. Presently, calories available per capita per day amount to some 3,000 in most of the developed countries. Total calories per capita per day, including domestic production and imported food, amount to about 2,000 in India and the Philippines, little more than 2,000 in Pakistan and Ceylon.

Problems of food and hunger go along with the persistence of traditional societies and high rates of human reproduction. Birth rates in Europe, the USSR, the United States, Oceania, and Japan are twenty-five or less per 1,000 total population. Birth rates in the Asian, Latin American, and African regions are forty or more per 1,000 total population. There is little overlap among the more and the less fortunate regions.

Death rates that were once high have been reduced substantially, but there is still a gap between levels in modernized and in traditional regions. In many individual countries, though, death rates have been reduced to very low levels without social and economic modernization. National and international public health activities are concentrating on the further reductions of mortality in those countries where deaths remain higher than they need be. The motivations and the achievements are commendable. But still declining death rates and still increasing rates of population growth complicate the problems of food and facilities.

Insufficient food, high birth rates, and rapid rates of population growth are associated both with major reliance on agriculture as a source of work and with the gross inadequacy of income. The developed countries have small proportions of the labor force in primary production, and primary production is a small proportion of gross domestic product. Major commitment to agriculture involves low per capita income along with a continuing insufficiency of food. Population growth intensifies the difficulties of the low income countries. Disproportionate numbers of earth's children are born in those areas where physical conditions of living are minimal. These are also the countries where opportunities for education and individual development are limited.

Time and Solutions

Growth is a continuing process. Today's growth is a product of the past. It is also the heritage of the future. This is obvious. Persons reaching age sixty-five this year were born in the nineteenth century. This year's surviving infants will reach age sixty-five in the third decade of the twenty-first century. Today's young men in the conscript ages of eighteen to twenty-one were born in the war years from 1942 to 1945. The survivors of the births of 1963 will reach age eighteen in 1981. Declines in birth rates cannot solve all problems of numbers immediately, or indeed for a very long period of time.[1] But problems of numbers will not be solved in the long run without declines in birth rates.

If there are to be declines in birth rates in the future, there will have to be advances in the age at marriage and control of conception among the married. Is it likely, then, that birth rates will decline? The answer is yes. Families and communities see the problems of their increasing numbers. National governments realize that there are major problems in economic development unless rates of population growth are solved. Many countries are making plans to educate people and to make knowledge of and facilities for contraception available in public health services.

Is the outlook for the future then optimistic? Will population problems be "solved" in the near future by declines in birth rates? The answer here is negative. There are no immediate solutions to problems of population growth, nor can there be any. Many decades of growth and a very considerable multiplication of numbers are inherent in the future, whatever the policies to reduce births and however speedy their influences.

There are two approaches to the problems of population. One is social and economic development; there must be improved living for people now alive. The other is demographic. There must be declines in birth rates if economic development is to become a continuing process. Given the acuteness of the problems in Asia, Africa, and Latin America today, the question is not a choice of approaches but a strategic combination of approaches and activities.

Our task is the survey of the facts and problems of growth. Such a survey presents a diverse picture of peoples, cultures and regions in which population and problems are so closely intertwined that the two words are used as one. This suggests again that population growth is not an isolated problem. It is, instead, one of the problems that in their entirety make for movement or stagnation, peace or war, survival or annihilation.

[1] The contributions of those declining birth rates to the economic developments that may be stimulants to further reductions in birth rates are noted in Chapter 4, "Population and Economic Development."

DEMOGRAPHY AND DEVELOPMENT

Discussion of underdeveloped areas implies a separation of the developed, the developing, and the underdeveloped. Such a separation of nations is invidious. All nations and all peoples seem to be travelling the same long route. They simply move at varying speeds. Nations may, however, be divided on the basis of the levels of birth and death rates. When this is done, there is also a classification of nations according to levels of living. This, in turn, is a classification of nations according to the status of economic and social advance.

Today most of earth's peoples may be placed in one of two categories, the demographically developed and the demographically underdeveloped. The distance between the two seems to be widening. When birth and death rates were alike tied to levels of living, there was a continuum of growth patterns from rapid increase through medium and slow increase to erratic stability and decline. This continuum was once viewed as a transition through which all peoples would pass. But this view is not supported by current developments. Presently, there are nations whose populations are increasing rapidly, and there are nations whose populations are increasing slowly. There are few underdeveloped nations in the intermediate ranges.

This demographic polarization has the most serious implications for the underdeveloped peoples. Poverty, malnutrition, illiteracy, social retardation, and political instability are clustered together in the countries with high birth rates. High incomes, abundant vitality, increasing professional and technical manpower, rapid social advance, and general political stability are clustered together in the countries with low or relatively low birth rates. Population growth compounds the difficulties of peoples whose modernization lies in the future. The ancient ways of living preserve the high rates of growth. Poverty perpetuates the conditions that preserve poverty. Population growth perpetuates the conditions that lead to population growth.

The problem of development is a total problem. It is futile to argue about *the* cause of poverty or slow development. It is the association of all factors that makes the problem of development so difficult. If one barrier to advance could be transformed into a factor for advance, the outlook would be bright. If there were rapid economic growth, the advancing levels of living would stimulate declining birth rates. If there were widespread education, social and economic movements would be simpler. If there were internal stability and international order, energies and resources now wasted could be utilized for development.

The close connection between economic, social, political and demographic processes is self-evident. Why emphasize population growth as a critical deterrent to modernization? Most of the peoples of history have had brief and limited lives. Why should men become restless because they cannot move into the late twentieth century in a few decades? The answer is obvious; it lies in the population growth that is occurring. Balance in modernization could once be defined as slow movement in all factors. No priorities could be assigned to population growth. Today death rates are relatively low and declining. This is true whether economies are developing, unchanging, or stagnating. Balance in modernization requires swift and continuing declines in birth rates to parallel the declines in death rates.

If the argument is valid, the reduction of population growth should have a priority in national and international activities as high as that given economic development itself. This conclusion may seem unrealistic today. It is likely to become an accepted principle in developmental planning within a few decades.

National and international work in the population field has increased consistently in the postwar years. Many nations have specific activities to induce their people to limit births. Other nations are considering work in this sphere. The publications of the United Nations Food and Agriculture Organization emphasize the problems of the increasing numbers of people. The activities of the Economic Commission for Asia and the Far East make the population problems of the region apparent to all. The Asian Population Conference of December of 1963 is indicative of the increasing concerns of the governments of the region.

The work of the United Nations in the population field has emphasized the collection of statistics and the analysis of population growth and its interrelations. There is movement toward cooperation in action programs, but the decision for cooperation has not yet been made. The first major consideration of birth control itself occurred in late 1962. The issues of international population policy and the development of national policies are considered in Chapters 7 and 8.

GROWTH IN THE TWENTIETH CENTURY

The population problems that underlie the developments of national and international policy are severe indeed. Estimates of the past and projections of the future underline the seriousness of the problems of the increasing populations (Table 1). These estimates were made in the early fifties. They now seem minimal. No allowances were made for the readjustment of China's historic population estimates. Moreover, actual growth in most underdeveloped areas has been substantially greater than that estimated prior to the censuses centered around the year 1960.

The differences between developed and underdeveloped nations are striking. There is growth in the developed sector, but it proceeds slowly.

TABLE I

Population growth in the twentieth century

Year	Developed[2]	Underdeveloped			
		Total	Asia[3]	Latin America	Africa
		Population (in millions[4])			
1900..................	554	996	813	63	120
1925..................	700	1,207	961	99	147
1950..................	838	1,659	1,297	163	199
1975..................	1,115	2,741	2,107	303	331
2000..................	1,448	5,459	4,145	651	663
		Per cent increase			
1900-1925..............	26.4	21.2	18.2	57.1	22.5
1925-1950..............	19.7	37.4	35.0	64.6	35.4
1950-1975..............	33.0	65.2	62.5	85.9	66.3
1975-2000..............	29.9	99.2	96.7	114.8	100.3
		Per cent of earth's total			
1900..................	35.7	64.3	52.4	4.1	7.7
1925..................	36.7	63.3	50.4	5.2	7.7
1950..................	33.6	66.4	51.9	6.5	8.0
1975..................	28.9	71.1	54.6	7.9	8.6
2000..................	21.0	79.0	60.0	9.4	9.6

[2] Including Europe, USSR, Northern America, Australia, New Zealand, and Japan.

[3] Excluding the Asian portion of the USSR and Japan.

[4] Enumerated or estimated, 1900-1950; projected, 1975 and 2000, high estimates,
Source (with modifications): United Nations Department of Economic and Social Affairs, *The Future Growth of World Population.* Table 5, p. 23, Population Studies No. 28. New York, 1958.

Growth in the underdeveloped sector was initially lower than that in the developed sector, but the rate moves continually upward.

The populations of the underdeveloped regions as a group increased by only one-fifth in the first quarter of the twentieth century. Their populations may double in the last quarter of the century. If this is the path of the century, the populations of the underdeveloped regions will have increased from one billion in 1900 to almost five and one-half billion in 2000.

While populations grow in inverse relation to their status in modernization, the populations of the underdeveloped regions constitute in-

creasing proportions of the earth's total. Developed areas had more than
one-third of the earth's total population in 1900. Under the assumptions
of the projections, they will have little more than one-fifth at the century's
end.

Toward 1975

The implications of population trends are clearer if analysis is
limited to the next ten or fifteen years. The number of people who will
exist in 1975 can be estimated with reasonable accuracy, provided only
that death rates remain at present levels or continue to move downward. No future declines in birth rates can reduce the numbers of the
people already born. And all persons who will reach age twelve or over
by 1975 are already born. Hence we shall discuss trends from 1960 to
1975.[5]
Consideration of numbers and the growth of numbers in developed
and underdeveloped countries are strangely impersonal. Hence we shall
consider the populations of six nations: Mexico and Brazil in Latin
America; Indonesia, Pakistan, and India in the accessible portions of
Asia; and the intricate enigma that can neither be analyzed nor ignored,
the Peoples Republic of China (Table 2).
Are the populations in 1960 and 1975, and the rates of growth from
the one date to the other, data that may be taken as firm with high degrees of probability? The answer is difficult. The populations enumerated
in the censuses of the years around 1960 were generally higher than official estimates or projections. The reasons are many, but in most countries the rate of decline in mortality and hence the rate of population
growth had been underestimated. What, then, about the path to 1975?
Death rates may decline more rapidly than assumed if conditions are
favorable. Or death rates may fail to decline or even increase if conditions
are not favorable.
The major uncertainty is the population of China. A registration
and investigation of the population by the People's Republic in late 1953
and early 1954 yielded a total of 582 million for the mainland area. *If*
the birth rate was 41.6 and the death rate 20.4, and *if* the death rate declined in the general Asian pattern while the birth rate remained unchanged, population increased from 582 million in 1953 to 733 million in

[5] This section is based on or abstracted from two regional papers, "Asian Population: The Critical Decades," U. S. House of Representatives, Committee on the Judi-
ciary, Subcommittee No. 1, *Study of Population and Immigration Problems*, Special
Series No. 4, Washington, D. C., Govt. Printing Office, 1962, 31 pp; "Population Growth:
Paradox of Development," National Conference on International Economic and Social
Development, Ninth Conference, *The Alliance for Progress*, Chicago, Ill., July 19-20,
1962.

TABLE 2

Projected total populations 1960 and 1975

| Countries | Population (in '000) | | Increase | |
	1960	1975**	Amount (in '000)	Per cent
Mexico......................	34,119	54,462	20,343	59.6
Brazil.......................	66,085	98,297	32,212	48.7
Indonesia...................	93,344	137,376	44,032	47.2
Pakistan*...................	95,387	145,630	50,243	52.7
India*......................	423,600	600,600	177,000	41.8
Mainland China*............	732,900	1,112,700	379,800	51.8

* Pakistan and India, 1961-1976; Mainland China, data of 1953 extended to 1963 and then projected to 1978.

** High projections.

Sources: United Nations Department of Social Affairs, Population Division, "Future Population Estimates by Sex and Age," *Report I: The Population of Central America 1950-1980* (Mexico) Table 2, p. 42, New York, 1954. *Report II: The Population of South America, 1950-1980* (Brazil) Table 4, p. 73, New York, 1955. United Nations Department of Economic and Social Affairs, *Report III: The Population of Southeast Asia, 1950-1980* (Indonesia) Table 6, pp. 138-139, New York, 1958. *Report IV: The Population of Asia and the Far East, 1950-1980* (Pakistan) Table xvii, p. 109; (India) Table viii, p. 100 (high fertility projection); (Mainland China) Table iv, p. 96 (low mortality, 1953 birth rate of 41.6), New York, 1959.

1963. *If* the population was 733 million in 1963 and trends continue until 1978, the population will exceed one billion.

The "ifs" with reference to the population of China are many. Perhaps the birth rate was higher or lower than 41.6 in 1953. Whatever it was, it is not likely that it was altered by the birth control controversies of recent years. Has it been influenced by disorganization and deprivation? What happened to the death rate during the period of the Great Leap Forward and the retreat? Indeed, what was the level of the death rate in 1953 and its course to 1958? The answers are simple. We do not know.

Total populations

The total populations, the amount of the population increase, and the percentages of that increase are given in Table 2. The numbers are great, and the increases are startling. Let us assume that initial estimates and terminal projections are accurate. If so, India must provide for an increase of 177 million within fifteen years. Pakistan's increase in the same period will be fifty million.

East Pakistan's population was estimated at fifty-three million in 1961; in 1976, under the assumed conditions, it will be eighty-four million. More than thirty million people will be added in a region without cities, industrial development, or known resources for industrialization. If this growth occurs, the people of East Pakistan will be settled 600 to the square kilometer. Quoting the conclusions of the United Nations study: "The problems of economic development posed by East Pakistan's rapidly growing population are of a kind and dimension hardly encountered in any other part of the world at this time." [6]

The population outlook for Indonesia is also dark. Present living is difficult. People are vulnerable to interruptions in food supply, whether episodically in crop failures or progressively in economic deterioration. However, if the mortality *should* decline to relatively lower levels, population *would* increase from ninety-three million in 1961 to 137 million in 1975.

The island of Java is a classic illustration of population growth. Lord Raffles estimated the population at four and one-half million in 1815. Even then there was concern over the pressures of people on the limited land. In 1960 there were more than sixty million people on the island of Java. If growth continues as projected, the population of this single island will exceed one hundred million by 1975. Whether the economy can absorb forty-four million additional people in the coming fifteen years is debatable. Population transfers from crowded Java to the relatively empty outer island may be palliative, but population transfers cannot be solutions.

In relative terms, the populations of the Asian nations were increasing in similar fashion in the past and, given continuities in development, they will do so in the future. Projected growth in the next fifteen years ranges from a low of forty-two per cent in India to a high of fifty-three per cent in Pakistan. The hypothetical progression of Mainland China to its population of more than a billion in 1978 involves rates of growth comparable to those assumed for the other underdeveloped countries.

Rapid and accelerated growth continues in Latin America. Under the assumed conditions of unchanging fertility and declining mortality, Mexico's population will increase three-fifths to reach fifty-four million in 1975, Brazil's population will increase almost one-half to approach one hundred million. Increases of similar orders of magnitude are occurring in agricultural areas where land reform is being planned on the basis of manpower now present. They are occurring in cities where present manpower is utilized most inefficiently; they are occurring in areas where resources are abundant as in areas where resources are limited. They are occurring in countries where economies are stable or retrogress-

[6] *The Population of Asia and the Far East, 1950-1980*, p. 14.

ing, as in countries where per capita income is increasing. They are occurring in countries where land is held in *hacienda, fundo,* or *estancia.* They are also occurring in Mexico, where revolution is ancient, *ejido* long established, and economic growth rapid.

The productive ages

Is it correct to assume that rates of population growth of forty to fifty per cent within a fifteen-year period constitute major population problems in these Asian and Latin American countries? The answer is an unequivocal yes! In Table 3, populations in the productive ages from fifteen to fifty-nine are given for the years 1960 and 1975, together with increases in numbers and rates of increase in this period.

TABLE 3

Populations in the productive ages 1960 and 1975

| Countries | Population Aged 15-59 (in '000) | | Increase | |
	1960	1975	Amount (in '000)	Per cent
Mexico...................	17,210	27,091	9,881	57.4
Brazil....................	35,125	50,963	15,838	45.1
Indonesia................	51,521	72,289	20,768	40.3
Pakistan.................	50,137	74,036	23,899	47.7
India....................	233,300	316,600	83,300	35.7
Mainland China...........	376,800	551,300	174,500	46.3

Notes and Sources: See Table 2.

The span of years from age fifteen through fifty-nine is a long one. The activities of men in these years are defined as labor, whatever the culture. This labor may involve working in the fields, in iron and steel works, or in the service and distribution sectors of traditional societies. The activities of women are more diverse, for these are the years that include marriage, homemaking, childbearing, and childrearing. On the whole, men and women in the central forty-five years of the lifespan provide economic support for persons in the younger and the older ages, as well as for themselves. They produce the younger generation for which they provide. And then they also support the aging and the aged.

The manpower increases presented in Table 3 for Mexico and Brazil show a projected increase of fifty-seven per cent for Mexico and forty-five per cent for Brazil. In these and the other countries of Central America and Tropical South America, manpower in the productive ages

40 *Irene B. Taeuber*

is increasing with extraordinary rapidity. And these years from 1960 to 1975 are the formative ones so important for the Alliance for Progress.

Women and families

In the years from 1960 to 1975 girls in their 'teens will increase by fifty per cent or more in the underdeveloped countries. If marriage ages and marriage frequencies remain unchanged, new families formed in 1975 will be half again more numerous than those formed in 1960. Given equal rates of childbearing, numbers of births in the late seventies will be half again more numerous than in the early sixties. It should be noted that this does not imply a rise in fertility. It is an increase in numbers due to the fact that more women are marrying and having children at the same rates.

Education

Numbers of children in elementary school ages are also increasing (Table 4). Given the accuracy of the projections, there are a hundred

TABLE 4

Children in elementary school ages 1960 and 1975

Countries	Population Aged 5-15 (in '000)		Increase	
	1960	1975	Amount	Per cent
Mexico....................	9,181	14,635	5,454	59.4
Brazil.....................	16,701	25,809	9,108	54.5
Indonesia..................	21,363	34,666	13,303	62.3
Pakistan...................	24,323	38,752	14,429	59.3
India......................	100,100	150,300	50,200	50.1
Mainland China............	182,800	292,700	109,900	60.1

Notes and Sources: See Table 2.

million children aged five to fourteen in India now. There will be one hundred fifty million fifteen years from now. Pakistan's twenty-four million children will increase to almost forty million, Indonesia's twenty-one million to thirty-five million. China's 180 million children of 1963 will increase to almost 300 million by 1978. The increase in children of elementary school ages in India, Pakistan, Indonesia, and Mainland China amount to 187 million in the years from 1960 to 1975.

Under the assumed conditions, numbers of children aged five to fourteen increase 5.5 million in Mexico, 9.1 million in Brazil. These numbers are small in comparison with those for the Asian countries. Rates of increase are equally rapid, however, and problems are almost equally acute.

In 1975, children now below age five will be aged fifteen to nineteen. The numbers of youth in the late 'teens and the increases in their numbers are given in Table 5. If the young men and women who will be

TABLE 5

Youth aged 15-19, 1960 and 1975

| | Number (in '000) | | Increase | |
Countries	1960	1975	Amount (in '000)	Per cent
Mexico.....................	3,402	5,657	2,255	66.3
Brazil.....................	6,574	10,125	3,551	54.0
Indonesia.................	8,416	14,275	5,859	69.6
Pakistan...................	9,517	15,035	5,518	58.0
India......................	41,500	60,000	18,500	44.6
Mainland China...........	62,000	113,500	51,500	83.1

Notes and Sources: See Table 2.

aged fifteen to nineteen in 1975 could all be educated, modernization could be accepted as a probability for the future. If the youth of 1975 are not educated, the workers and the parents of the following decades will not be educated. If they are not, the struggles against the many problems of ill-trained human resources will continue for still another generation.

The advance of education is perhaps the single most critical factor beyond economic viability itself. The self-perpetuating mechanisms of societies are nowhere more apparent and more serious than here. The large families are part of a complex of forces that preserve traditionalism and illiteracy. These in turn preserve the early marriages, the frequent childbearing, and the high rates of population growth.

SOME CULTURAL DIMENSIONS

There is a general awakening to the significance of population growth as a major problem in the underdeveloped areas. Resolution of the difficulties involves two processes. The first is economic and social development to provide improving levels of living for people now alive. The second is declines in birth rates. The speed with which individual countries move toward solutions depends partially on resources and present states of technologies. It also depends on the characteristics and drives of the people themselves. The idea of change and the means to achieve it may be introduced from elsewhere. Change itself is indigenous.

Technologies of death control were introduced as simple procedures, and they spread quickly. Deep desires for longer life existed among all people, whatever the culture or the state of development. Technologies of birth control cannot be introduced as simple and universally applicable procedures. Once introduced, there are barriers to swift diffusion and hazards to effective use.

There is no universal goal to insure continuing declines in birth rates. In this area of decision and action, as in economic and social change in general, there are major differences among peoples. Readiness for development and effective design in development plans differ widely from country to country. There are awakened aspirations and aroused expectations among all peoples, but probabilities of development differ widely.

Today almost all underdeveloped peoples have high birth rates, reduced death rates, and high rates of population growth. But how high are high birth rates? In what ways and to what extents are they resistant to change? How low are death rates, and how precarious are the balances of subsistence and people? How strong are the motivations for cultural survival and national development among elites and masses? How extensive is knowledge of the relation of population growth to national development and individual advance? How effective is leadership in the localities where families live and bear the children that are the family's pride and the nation's problem?

There has been much generalization in the preceding sections. Population problems are not solved in general but in specific situations. Analysis of the particular settings in many countries is not possible here. There may be some approach to realism if the population outlooks are related to the cultures.

The expansion of European peoples throughout the underdeveloped areas was an expansion of Christian culture. Birth rates were declining in Europe, and they declined among European peoples overseas. The general impact on the other peoples involved stability or increase in birth rates, not decline. There are classic instances of rising birth rates in the Micronesian Islands. Here missionaries defined native mores as sinful. High birth rates followed the religious conversions. In vast portions of Mainland Asia, practices that had long existed came to be regarded as backward, if not indeed barbarian. Infanticide and exposure declined. The remarriage of widows became more frequent. Concubinage became less frequent. Then, too, improving nutrition and better health led to increasing birth rates. The process is not yet ended. In some areas birth rates may rise still higher before they begin to decline.

It should be emphasized again that the normal level of the birth rates in the underdeveloped areas is and has always been high. The present rates of growth are due almost entirely to reductions in death rates. The point here is that whatever influence Western contact exerted on fertility was likely to lead to increase. Peoples who were controlling their own fertility did not concern themselves with the problems of high fertility elsewhere. Ideals of mortality control were spread assiduously; ideals of fertility control were not.

Neither fertility nor mortality have been uniform in levels or in changes among regions, peoples, and cultures. In the future, mortality is likely to continue to move downward as health services are extended. The only barrier to continuing decline would be a serious failure in economic advance. Fertility is likely to move downward, but not at uniform and easily predictable rates among all peoples. Increasing diversities in levels of birth rates are likely to exist for a considerable period of time. Cursory survey of the underdeveloped areas of the world is likely to be a far more intricate task at the century's end than it is today.

There are no simple ways to predict future declines in fertility. The resistances to reduced family size might be expected to be highest in the Latin American countries and the Philippines. There are major components of an indigenous base in population and culture. Resources will permit appreciable growth without the threat of starvation. Religion is Catholic. But in South America, Argentina and Uruguay have fairly low birth rates, and Chile's rate is intermediate. Catholicism was not inconsistent with early decline and persistent low levels of fertility in European countries. It may not be inconsistent with rapid decline in non-European settings.

The central population problem of the world is the Asian one. In this area diversities in paths to and speed of transition are already apparent. Japan's record has been phenomenal in speed of industrialization, urbanization, public education, and comprehensive modernization. Fertility is now reduced to such low levels that it is insufficient for permanent replacement. There are suggestions of reduced or declining fertility in Taiwan and Hong Kong and among the Chinese in Singapore.

The faith and culture of Islam are perhaps most conducive to high fertility. The ethical ideals, the family values, and the roles assigned to women are all structured to maximize fertility. And fertility is high indeed in the great crescent from North Africa through Malaya and on eastward to Indonesia and north to Mindanao. However, Egypt and Pakistan are developing plans and activities to stimulate family planning. Other Islamic countries are considering problems and policies.

The most difficult of all population problems are those of nonliterate peoples suddenly sovereign in a complex environment for which they are ill prepared. In the scattered islands of the vast Pacific solutions other than education and out-migration are difficult to envision. However, Hawaii stands as a world symbol of the potentialities of all Oceanic and Asian peoples to achieve advanced modernization within one or two generations.

The demographic outlook for much of sub-Saharan Africa is difficult to envision in other than pessimistic focus. Given political stability, feasible developments seem to lie along the lines of creating stable and largely subsistence agricultural populations. If so, the demographic path might seem to lead toward Asian-type population pressures and rates of population growth. But Asian subsistence agriculture involves high levels of discipline and skill among the cultivators and their families. Land division and utilization without those disciplines and skills may have most serious consequences, not only for today's peoples but for the basic resources of forest, land, and water that are the heritage for future generations.

Projections of populations into the future on specific assumptions are simple in concept and execution. Such projections indicate the hazards inherent in the long future unless birth rates decline. But what will be the populations of the future—in Latin America, in Monsoon Asia, in Islamic North Africa and the Middle East, in sub-Saharan Africa? Will Brazil, the Indian nations of the Andean highlands, and Mexico move along the same paths? Can one assume uniform futures for Indonesia, India, and Pakistan? And what of the greatest of all questions, the present and the future of the population of Mainland China? Demographers and sociologists must yield to seers if there are to be answers to questions such as these.

ASPIRATIONS AND RESOLUTIONS

Perhaps the greatest social and political process of our times is the development of aspirations among the ordinary peoples of Latin America, Asia, and Africa. The corollary of aspirations in a milieu of population growth, precarious economic advance, and rigidity in social structures is frustration.

Instability, subversion, and revolution are associated with frustrated advance. They also serve to retard the advance that is desired. The role of population pressure and population growth is simple to demonstrate through the citation of illustrations. It is also simple to demonstrate the lack of relevance through the citation of alternate illustrations. If population growth is a factor in economic failure, it is also a factor in the resulting political instabilities.

The policies and plans of nations involve many phrases of economic development and social change. Land reform, education, and the extension of opportunities are pervasive motifs. Some countries include plans for reducing birth rates along with economic and social measures. Neither the Alliance for Progress nor the United Nations and its specialized agencies have yet achieved this level of balanced realism.

The direct relevance of ideology to population trends is debatable. Not so long ago there were two major ideologies. There was the philosophy labelled Malthusianism. A deeply pessimistic view of man's propensity to increase his numbers was combined with a naively optimistic view of the miraculous results that could be achieved if governments and peoples would approve birth control. Then there was the Marxist-Leninist ideology. Here men were regarded as consumers. In this argument population problems would vanish under scientific forms of social organization.

The ideological confrontations continue, but at diminishing tempo. In countries where Malthusianism once prevailed, theories of demographic transition were developed to explain trends toward declining vital rates and slowing population growth. In Communist countries where Marxism-Leninism once prevailed in classic form, there are theories of population trends appropriate to forms of social organization. Ideologies are factors, but they too are shifting aspects of rapidly shifting demographic views (See Chapter 8).

Neither forms of economic organization nor political ideologies barred declining birth rates in modernizing countries. Political ideologies have altered in underdeveloped countries, but population problems have not been solved thereby. The greatest of the examples is the People's Republic of China, where death remains the major variable and chief determinant of growth.

Our task ends with the statement of facts. Questions of policy and solution are the topics of later chapters.

Ansley J. Coale

4

Population and Economic Development

Anyone examining estimates of per capita incomes or other indexes of material well-being must be impressed with the wide difference —by a factor of ten or more—between the wealthiest and the poorest countries. The countries with the highest average incomes are those that have undergone industrialization or modernization; and the countries with lowest incomes are those that retain traditional techniques of production and modes of industrial organization (with a predominance of agriculture in most instances) that have persisted without essential change for generations. The disparity between the prosperity of the industrialized countries and the poverty of the pre-industrial countries is an increasing irritant to the pride and ambition of the leaders in the underdeveloped areas and to the conscience of the modernized countries.

It is the purpose of this chapter to consider how the demographic characteristics of the low-income countries are related to their poverty, and how their population trends will influence their modernization. Other chapters in this book have described the nature of the population in the underdeveloped areas of the world and current population trends in these areas. Among the demographic characteristics of low income areas today are:

High fertility—Most underdeveloped areas of the world have birth rates of forty per 1000 or higher and an average number of children born at the end of the fertile period—at age of forty-five or fifty—of at least 5. This fertility contrasts with experience in Europe, where birth rates are,

ANSLEY J. COALE *is Professor of Economics and Director, Office of Population Research, Princeton University. He serves currently as United States Representative on the Population Commission of the United Nations. He is Second Vice President of the Population Association of America and a Fellow of the American Statistical Association. Among his publications (with E. M. Hoover) is* Population Growth and Economic Development in Low Income Countries.

with only two or three exceptions, below twenty per 1,000, and total fertility is two to three children. The fertility of Japan is at the low end of the European scale. Other highly industrialized areas outside of Europe—the United States, the Soviet Union, Australia, New Zealand and Canada —have birth rates between twenty and twenty-eight per 1,000 and a total fertility of three to four children.

Low or rapidly falling mortality—As a consequence of the invention and application of low cost techniques of public health, underdeveloped areas have recently experienced a fall in mortality more rapid than ever seen before. They have not had to wait while the gradual process of developing medical science took place; nor have they had to depend on the possibly more rapid but still difficult process of constructing major sanitary engineering works and building up of a large inventory of expensive hospitals, public health services and highly trained doctors. Instead, the underdeveloped areas have been able to import low-cost measures of controlling disease, measures developed for the most part in the highly industrialized countries. The use of residual insecticides to provide effective protection against malaria at no more than twenty-five cents per capita per year is an outstanding example. Other innovations include antibiotics and chemo-therapy, and extend to the discovery of relatively low-cost ways of providing a safe water supply and adequate environmental sanitation in villages that in other ways remain little touched by modernization.

Accelerating population growth—The result of a precipitous decline in mortality while the birth rate remains essentially unchanged is, of course, a rapid acceleration in population growth, reaching in some instances rates of three to three and one-half per cent per year. The underdeveloped areas with more moderate growth rates of one and one-half to two and one-half per cent per year are typically in the midst of a rapid decline in death rates, and are experiencing steep increases in the rate of growth of their populations.

A very young age distribution—The high fertility of low-income countries produces a large proportion of children and a small proportion, in consequence, of adults in the economically most productive ages. The underdeveloped countries have forty to forty-five per cent of their population under age fifteen, in contrast with a maximum of twenty-five to thirty per cent in the highly industrialized countries. Differences in mortality among countries, whether industrialized or not, have only slight effect on the distribution of the population by age, and specifically on the proportion of the population that children constitute. Indeed, the effect of a lower death rate on the proportion of children is in a surprising direction. Mortality is typically reduced the most in infancy and early childhood; and if fertility remains unchanged, a reduction in mortality of the sort usually occurring increases the proportion of children and reduces rather than increases the average age.

Density ranging from low to high—There are great variations in population density from one low-income area to another, with fewer than ten persons per square mile in Bolivia, and more than 600 in Korea.

In this chapter we shall consider how these characteristics of the population affect the process of industrialization or modernization to which the low income areas aspire. Their populations at present suffer from inadequate diets, enjoy at best primitive and overcrowded housing, have a modest education or no formal education at all (if adult) and rarely attend school (if children), and are often productively employed for only a fraction of the year. These populations suffer all of the misery and degradation associated with poverty. They naturally wish to enjoy the universal education, adequate diet, housing equipped with modern amenities, the long and generally healthy life, the opportunity for productive work and extensive voluntary leisure that the highly industrialized countries have shown to be possible. To do so the underdeveloped countries must modernize their economies.

The changes in social and economic structure that make up the process of modernization or industrialization are many and profound. More productive techniques must displace traditional methods of manufacturing, agriculture, trade, transport and communications. Economic activity must become more diversified and more specialized. The emphasis in production must shift from extractive industries, especially agriculture, to manufacturing, trade and communications. The interchange of goods through a monetary medium on widespread markets must replace local consumption of goods produced on the farm or exchanged only in small village markets. The labor force must be transformed from illiteracy to literacy. A sufficient supply must be found and trained of what has become to be known as "high talent manpower"—doctors, lawyers, engineers, entrepreneurs and managers. Production must shift from small, family-oriented enterprises into large, impersonal, professionally supervised organizations. However, many of these essential changes are related only indirectly to demographic characteristics such as growth and age distribution.

To explore in detail these indirect relationships would go far beyond the scope of this chapter. Here only two important aspects of industrialization or modernization will be considered. One aspect is increasing income per person as a consequence (and an index) of industrialization, and the other is the attainment or maintenance of productive employment for the labor force.

POPULATION AND INCOME PER HEAD

Examining the implications of population change for the growth of real income we shall consider nations rather than areas within nations.

The selection of the nation as the unit for analysis implies that gains or losses of population through migration can generally be considered of negligible importance. There are a few exceptions (perhaps four or five small countries that can expect gains or losses from migration of important magnitude compared to natural increase), but for the majority of underdeveloped countries and certainly for the larger ones there is no such realistic likelihood.

For somewhat different reasons, the possibility of alternative courses of mortality can also be ignored, at least for a generation or two. The basis for paying little attention to different possible courses of mortality is that the technical feasibility of reducing mortality to lower levels—of increasing expectation of life at birth at least to some fifty or sixty years— has been widely demonstrated in the underdeveloped areas themselves. Unless the effort to start and continue the process of modernization fails completely, or unless there is a breakdown in world order, the attainment and maintenance, at least for a short time, of low mortality rates seems potentially within the reach of most low-income countries. It does not appear that widespread famine or even severe increases in malnutrition are a necessary consequence in the next few decades, even if the low-income countries experience population growth rates of two to three and one-half per cent.

The agricultural and industrial technology that can be introduced into low-income countries is, in a sense, parallel to the medical technology that can be imported to achieve a rapid reduction in mortality rates. Rates of increase in agricultural output of at least three or four per cent a year appear technically feasible, even in such a densely settled, highly agricultural country as India. If the birth rate in India is not reduced, the population will probably double in the next generation from about 450 million to about 900 million persons. Agricultural experts consider it feasible within achievable limits of capital investment to double Indian agricultural output within the next twenty or twenty-five years. In the short run, then, it can be assumed, provisionally at least, that mortality reduction can be achieved and maintained.

Finally, if sickness can be reduced and death postponed within the resources available to the health authorities in the underdeveloped countries, assisted by the World Health Organization, UNICEF, and directly by the industrialized countries, it is scarcely imaginable that by deliberate policy these opportunities would be foregone. In other words, the only factor that can be realistically considered as variable in causing population change by deliberate policy is fertility. We shall be concerned here with the implications, for the growth in per capita income and for the provision of productive employment, of alternative possible future courses of fertility. The specific alternatives to be considered are the maintenance of fertility at its current level (which would involve in almost all underdeveloped countries the continuation of an essentially horizontal trend that has already continued for generations) and, as the contrasting alternative, a rapid reduction in fertility, amounting to fifty per cent of the initial level and occupying a transitional period of about twenty-five years.

We will inquire what effects these contrasting trends in fertility would have on three important population characteristics: first, the burden of dependency, defined as the total number of persons in the population divided by the number in the labor force ages (fifteen to sixty-four); second, the rate of growth of the labor force, or, more precisely, the annual per cent rate of increase of the population fifteen to sixty-four; and third, the density of the population, or, more precisely, the number of persons at labor force age relative to land area and other resources. Then we shall consider how these three characteristics of dependency, rate of growth, and density influence the increase in per capita income.

Alternative population projections

It is possible to translate assumptions about the future course of mortality and fertility in a specific population into numerical estimates of the future size and age composition of that population. Table 1 presents the projection one hundred fifty years into the future of a hypothetical initial population of one million persons with an age distribution and

TABLE I

Illustrative Projections of the Population of an Underdeveloped Area

(Initial population 1,000,000 persons. Initial age distribution, fertility, and mortality typical of Latin America north of Uruguay. Mortality rapidly improving.)

Projection A—Fertility continues unchanged.
Projection B—Fertility falls linearly by fifty per cent in twenty-five years, thereafter unchanged.

Population in Thousands

	Year	0	10	20	30	40	50	60	150
Projection A	0-14	434	616	870	1,261	1,840	2,655	3,848	110,700
	15-64	534	718	996	1,406	2,003	2,901	4,204	120,800
	65+	32	43	65	90	132	180	245	14,000
	Total	1,000	1,377	1,931	2,757	3,975	5,736	8,297	245,500
Projection B	0-14	434	567	637	676	783	901	994	3,014
	15-64	534	718	985	1,287	1,573	1,869	2,181	6,613
	65+	32	43	65	90	132	180	245	850
	Total	1,000	1,328	1,687	2,053	2,488	2,950	3,420	10,477

fertility and mortality rates typical of a Latin American country. The current birth rate is about forty-four per 1,000; the current death rate is about fourteen per 1,000, so that the population is growing at three per-cent per year. The current expectation of life at birth is about fifty-three years, and the average number of children born by age forty-five is slightly over six. It is assumed that in the next thirty years the expectation of life at birth will rise to approximately seventy years, so that mortality risks at each age become closely comparable to today's experience in the most highly industrialized countries. Once the expectation of life reaches seventy years, no further improvement is assumed. If this projection of one million persons is multiplied by 70.5, it would fit Brazil; by 34.6, it would fit Mexico, starting in 1960.

The initial population and the expected mortality risks at each age in the future are the same for the two projected populations. However, two contrasting assumptions are made with regard to the future course of fertility. In one projection, it is assumed that the current rates of child-bearing at each age of women continue indefinitely into the future. In the other projection, it is assumed that fertility rates are reduced each year for twenty-five years by two per cent of their initial value, so that in twenty-five years fertility is reduced by a total of fifty per cent. After twenty-five years, this projection is based on a continuation of fertility at fifty per cent of current levels. Note that there is no difference in the first fifteen years in the projected population over age fifteen. Differences in fertility such as are assumed between these alternative projected popu-lations inevitably affect the child population before the adult population is affected. In fact, at the end of twenty-five years, when fertility for one population has fallen by fifty per cent, the population fifteen to sixty-four is only four per cent greater in the high fertility projection. It is nine per cent greater after thirty years. In the more distant future the diver-gence becomes increasingly rapid. After about sixty-two years the high fertility population would have twice as many people in the labor force ages, and by 150 years it would have eighteen times as many.

The three population characteristics whose implications are to be examined here are of differing relative significance in the short run, over an intermediate period, and in the long run. In the first twenty-five or thirty years the age distribution effect, or the difference in burden of de-pendency, is almost the sole factor at work. There is a rapidly widening difference between the projected populations in the burden of depend-ency during the first generation (Figure 1). This difference in dependency once established then continues more or less unchanged. Starting in about twenty years there develops first a slight and then a widening dif-ference in the rate of growth of the population aged fifteen to sixty-four. This difference in rate of increase reaches a maximum value, at which it thereafter remains, in about sixty-five to seventy years (or forty to fifty years after fertility levels off). The period of widening differences in the

Ansley J. Coale

growth rate will be considered as an intermediate one separating the
short and the long run. The two projections have essentially constant
differences in age composition and rate of growth in the long run (from
sixty-five to seventy-five years on). During the intermediate period there

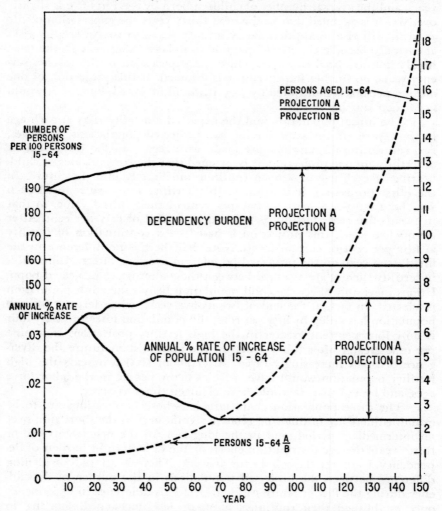

OFFICE OF POPULATION RESEARCH, PRINCETON UNIVERSITY

*Figure 1. Dependency burden (total number of persons 15-64); relative size of the
population 15-64; and annual rate of increase of population 15-64 in two model projections (Projection A, Fertility unchanged. Projection B, Fertility reduced linearly by
50% in 25 years, thereafter constant.)*

develops an increasingly conspicuous difference in the size of the two labor forces, and therefore in the density of the labor force relative to resources. In the long run the difference in density assumes overwhelming dimensions. For example, in something less than three hundred years the high fertility population would be a thousand times bigger than the low fertility population.

To sum up: In the short run there is a reduction in the burden of dependency in the low fertility relative to the high fertility population. This difference reaches a stable maximum in some thirty years. In addition to this effect there begins to develop in the intermediate period a widening difference in the rate of growth of the population of labor force age. This difference attains a maximum (thereafter maintained) within seventy years. The cumulative effect of differences in rates of growth of the labor force in the long run produce overwhelming differences between the high fertility and low fertility population in the size or density of the labor force.

Economic development and demographic variables

We shall consider primarily the implications of our demographic variables for the capacity of the economy to divert effort and resources from producing for current consumption to producing for the enhancement of future productivity. In other words, it will be assumed that to accelerate the process of modernization an economy must increase its level of net investment. Net investment here means additions to factories, roads, irrigation networks, fertilizer plants and other productive facilities. It also can include in a broad definition resources and effort devoted to education and training. It is not an intended implication that merely stepping up the rate of new investment automatically insures a major speed-up in industrialization, or assures the attainment of the fastest possible pace of modernization. Resources mobilized for productive purposes must be wisely allocated. Adequate leadership must be found for the new forms of productive organization that an industrialized society requires. Long-standing customs and traditions must be altered if new and more effective techniques of production are to be employed. In other words, a high level of net investment is a *necessary* but not a *sufficient* condition for a rapid pace of industrialization. In the ensuing analysis it will be assumed that the other crucial elements in modernization are present.

Age distribution and investment

At the end of twenty-five years there is only a four per cent difference in the size of the labor force or, more precisely, a four per cent difference in the number of persons fifteen to sixty-four. Let us suppose that productive employment can be found for all males of labor force age seeking employment and for all females who are not bound to house-keeping duties by lack of education, tradition, and the necessity to care for small children and who also are in search of productive employment. Let us assume further that twenty-five years from now the progress toward modernization has included the establishment of virtually universal primary education, so that the effective age of entry in the labor force is not before age fifteen. Let us also make the provisional assumption, whicb we shall re-examine shortly, that national income is, in the twenty-fifth year, the same for the two projected populations. If the reader objects that this provisional assumption seems unrealistic because the high fertility population would have some four per cent more persons of labor force age, let him consider the offsetting fact that the low fertility population would contain only about half as many young infants and half as many pregnant women. If allowance is made for the greater number of women free to work outside the home, the number of persons actually available for productive employment would not really be four per cent less in the low fertility population but might actually be slightly greater. It is certainly reasonable to disregard the small difference in size of population over age fifteen.

If there were the same total national income to be utilized by the two projected populations, the pressure toward utilizing nearly all of it for consumption would be substantially greater in the high fertility population, as a direct result of the greater burden of dependency that must be borne by the labor force. In the high fertility population after twenty-five years, there would be ninety-six persons in the dependent ages for every one hundred persons in the productive ages, while in the low fertility population there would be only sixty-five dependents for every one hundred persons fifteen to sixty-four.

The pressure to spend a higher fraction of national income on consumption can take many forms in different kinds of economies. In a capitalist economy, where investment is financed out of private savings, the fact that families with a large number of children find it more difficult to save reduces the volume of savings and hence the level of investment. When low-income families are not an important source of savings, higher fertility creates social pressure to increase the share of national income received by the poorest earners (the non-savers) in order to maintain minimum standards of consumption.

High fertility can depress private savings in two ways: (1) by reducing the volume of savings by individual families when such savings are an important component of the national total; (2) by increasing the proportion of national income that must accrue to non-savers if standards of consumption play any part in determining the earnings of low-income families.

When it is the government rather than individual entrepreneurs that provides a large proportion of national investment, fertility affects the level of investment through its effect on the c *i*pacity of the government to raise money through taxation. Suppose the government attempts to maximize the fund it mobilizes for net investment. For any given level of deprivation that it is prepared to impose, it can raise more taxes from a low fertility population than from a high fertility population with the same national income and the same number of adults in each. Even if the government does not calculate the maximum revenue it can assess, the existence of such factors as exemptions for children would automatically reduce income tax revenues.

After this lengthy review we reach a simple conclusion. Given the same labor force and the same total national income, a low fertility population will achieve a higher level of net investment than a high fertility population. It will therefore be able to make larger additions to the productive capacity of the country and achieve a higher national product in the next year. In addition, the population with a higher burden of child dependency feels a constant pressure to divert investment funds to less productive or at least to less immediately productive uses. To meet given target dates for achieving universal literacy or universal primary education, more funds must be spent on education. In a population of large families rather than small, more construction must be diverted to housing rather than to factories or hydroelectric plants.

During a short-run period of twenty-five to thirty years, the age-distribution effect of declining fertility enhances the capacity of the economy to increase its net investment, and to utilize investment in more immediately productive ways. The labor force available for productive employment during the short-run period is the same, or perhaps a little larger during the first fifteen years because persons over fifteen would be the same in number and more women could participate in productive employment. Actual numbers available for employment probably become equal in the two projections some time between twenty-five and thirty years after the decline of fertility starts. The resources available would presumably be identical. In consequence, there emerges a conclusion that may seem paradoxical. During a period of twenty-five or thirty years, at least, after fertility reduction begins, the population reducing its fertility would produce a more rapidly growing national product than a population which kept its fertility unchanged. This more rapid growth would cumulate into a consequentially higher total product at the end of the thirty-year period. In other words, in the short run not only does a population with reduced fertility enjoy the benefit of dividing the national product among a smaller number of consumers, it enjoys the additional benefit of having a larger national product to divide.

Effects of labor force growth

After twenty-five or thirty years declining fertility begins to cause major differences in the growth rate, and later on major differences in the size of the adult population. The difference in dependency burden reaches a maximum by about forty years, thereafter remaining unchanged. The high fertility labor force must continue, as in the short run, to share what it produces with a distinctly greater number of dependents, and this necessity continues to impair the capacity of the economy to attain a high level of investment. But after the short run a new element, the different rate of growth of the labor force itself, assumes important dimensions.

The significance of the growth of the labor force for income per head is that higher rates of growth imply a higher level of needed investment to achieve a given per capita output, although there is nothing about faster growth that generates a greater supply of investible resources. A larger labor force requires a larger stock of productive facilities in order to have the same productivity per head. The per cent of national income that must be invested merely to keep productivity from declining is some three times the annual per cent rate of increase of the labor force. In other words, if the labor force were growing by three per cent a year, a level of net investment of nine per cent of national income would be required to prevent declining productivity, while if the rate of growth of the labor force were one per cent a year, the needed level of investment for this purpose would be only three per cent of national income.

This rule of thumb assumes that the stock of capital must increase as much as the labor force to prevent a decline of productivity, and assumes further that the stock of capital is roughly three times as large as the current level of national income. Yet the faster growing labor force has no intrinsic advantages in achieving a high level of savings to finance the needed higher level of investment. It needs more investment but has inherent advantages in achieving more.

Another way of presenting the difference between a rapidly growing and a slowly growing labor force is to consider the effect of net investment at the respectable rate of fifteen per cent of national income. A population with a rate of growth of three per cent in its labor force can with such a level of net investment add about two per cent per year to the endowment of capital per worker. If the labor force were growing at one per cent, the annual increase in the stock of capital per worker would be four per cent.

An economy where additional members of the labor force settle on empty land, a "frontier society," is a partial exception to the above line of reasoning. If frontier settlement provides an outlet for the growth in the labor force, it is possible that new members provide most of their own capital—by clearing land, constructing roads, building log houses, etc. Under these hypothetical circumstances the rate of capital formation might be automatically higher with a more rapidly growing labor force. However, it is uncertain whether there are genuine instances of this kind of frontier settlement in the world today. Indonesia has attempted to resettle families from densely populated and rapidly growing Java to the relatively empty land in Borneo. However, the Indonesian government has felt impelled to make a generous capital investment in the form of tools and equipment for each family, the numbers involved have been at most a trivial fraction of the annual increase in Java's population, and many of the pioneers have returned to Java after a short period.

Most underdeveloped countries find it difficult to invest as much as fifteen per cent of their national incomes, and hence will find it necessary for the next generation to utilize more than half of their investment merely to provide capital for the growing labor force. In the short run a reduction of fertility would not affect this necessity. However, even in the short run the age distribution advantages of reduced fertility would increase the level of net investment that would be attained. During the intermediate period, when reduced fertility results in a substantially slower growth of the labor force, the age distribution advantage would continue. A greater capacity to allocate output to investment would be combined with a less imperative necessity to invest merely to keep up with the growth of the labor force.

Effect of density

The question of population density tends to be the dominant concept in most casual thought about the population problems of underdeveloped areas. The notion of excessive density is certainly implicit in the term "overpopulation." The underlying idea is that when there are too many workers relative to the available resources, per capita output is smaller than it would be with a smaller number of workers. Given gross enough differences in the numbers of workers being compared, it is certainly possible in principle to establish that overpopulation in this sense exists. For example, in 150 years the high fertility population that we projected would be eighteen times as large as the population that would result from fifty per cent reduction in fertility. Even the labor force with reduced fertility would imply a density more than twelve times greater than at present, while the population with sustained fertility would involve a density more than 200 times greater than at present. There is little doubt that in most countries a density 200 times greater would have a depressing effect upon per capita output compared to a density twelve times greater.

There are, however, two reasons for doubting the immediate usefulness of the concept of density in considering population problems of underdeveloped areas. The first is that in this period of human history few countries have any genuine freedom of choice of policy that would have an important effect on population density (or, more specifically, on the density of the labor force) in the short run. There are few areas where realistic alternatives of promoting or retarding international migration would have an important effect upon density. It is unlikely, and I would argue strongly undesirable, that an underdeveloped country should contemplate a deliberate restraint on its public health programs in order to retard the decline of mortality and thus prevent an increase of population density. As is shown in Figure 1, a reduction in fertility does not have an important effect on density for a long time in the future. The difference in the size of the labor force is less than ten per cent thirty years after a rapid and extensive decline and fertility begins. After thirty years, however, the difference in density between sustained and reduced fertility rapidly mounts, reaching a factor of two in about sixty years, a factor of three in seventy-five years, and a factor of eighteen after 150 years. In other words, so far as acceptable and attainable policies are concerned, only in the relatively distant future can the density of the labor force relative to resources be affected. In the meantime the policy that would have a long-run effect on density, namely one that reduces fertility, would through changes in dependency and differences in the annual rate of growth of the labor force have produced major economic effects.

A second reservation about the relevance of density is that it is of clearcut importance only in a closed economy—i.e., one that does not trade extensively—or in an economy where the principal industry is extractive. Only in extractive industries—mining, agriculture, and forestry—are resources as related to numbers of workers a dominant element in productivity. For example, if India were compelled to continue to employ seventy per cent of its labor force in agriculture, increasing density would inevitably mean smaller average holdings. The average holding today is only about two acres per person aged fifteen to sixty-four dependent on agriculture, and the possibility of bringing new areas under cultivation is limited.

In non-extractive industries international trade can greatly reduce the effect of limited resources. In all industries, extractive or otherwise, productivity is determined to a large degree by the stock of capital per worker. The underdeveloped areas have in common a small endowment of productive equipment per worker relative to the industrialized countries; in other words, the underdeveloped countries all have a "high density" of workers relative to capital, whether the country appears to be sparsely or densely settled relative to land and other resources.

Two examples indicate the dubious relevance of the concept of overpopulation where non-extractive industries are dominant and a large volume of trade is possible. One is the narrow strip of territory extending from Boston to Washington along the east coast of the United States. There is a 400 mile long line of contiguous counties with an aggregate area of about 14,000 square miles and an aggregate population in 1960 of about 28,000,000, or a population density of more than 2,000 per square mile. There are few if any areas of similar extent in the world with a higher density. The median family income of this strip is $6,660, just a thousand dollars more than the median for the United States as a whole. Is it overpopulated? It would certainly be difficult to demonstrate that per capita output would be greater if the population density were less. Of course this area belongs to a large market—the United States and its territories—where trade is unrestricted. Extractive industries play a trivial role in the output of this area. It can readily import the raw materials and semi-finished products that it requires in exchange for the finished goods and services it produces.

The second example, Hong Kong, shows that the possibility of importing raw materials and semi-finished goods in exchange for finished goods and services is not limited to a region within a country. Hong Kong has a population of 3.1 million on a land area of 398 square miles, with a resultant density of 12,700 persons per square mile. Land for new buildings on Victoria Island is dredged from the harbor. After the war Hong Kong had a very low per capita income, and its density was inflated by an influx of refugees. Nevertheless Hong Kong has achieved increases in national produce of seven to ten per cent per year and has probably doubled its real output in a decade. It obtains its needed imports (including food) on the world market. Mainland China has receded to a minor position in Hong Kong's pattern of trade, providing only seventeen per cent of Hong Kong's imports in 1961. Hong Kong has very important special advantages, especially in terms of human capital, as data from the 1961 census show. The refugees that swarmed into Hong Kong were not illiterate peasants but had an average educational attainment well above what must characterize China as a whole. Among the immigrants were experienced entrepreneurs from Shanghai. In short, Hong Kong was endowed with an energetic, literate and partially trained labor force and had no scarcity of organizational and entrepreneurial skills. It nevertheless remains a fact that an extraordinarily high density of population relative to resources has not prevented an extraordinarily rapid increase in per capita income.

In the normal course of industrialization the proportion of the population engaged in agriculture and other extractive industries steadily declines. In the history of every highly industrialized area a period was reached during which the number of persons dependent on agriculture was stabilized so that all increases in population of labor force age caused increases only in non-agricultural employment. The period of unchanging numbers engaged in agriculture has typically been followed by a shrinkage in the absolute number. This sequence has been typical both in countries where the initial density of agricultural settlement was very high, such as Japan, or where it was relatively low, as in the United States or New Zealand. The implications of this sequence for employment in industrializing countries will be considered later. Here its relevance is that for countries in the earlier stages of economic development some of the increases in the labor force must seek employment in extractive industries. If the agricultural population is already densely settled (as in India), this necessity undoubtedly constitutes a greater hardship or barrier to rapidly increasing incomes than in a less densely settled country.

As was noted earlier, the underdeveloped countries all suffer from what might be called a high density of population relative to *capital*. Therefore the effects not only of the age distribution but also of the rate of growth of the labor force (with their respective implications for the ease with which capital formation can proceed and for the rate at which it must proceed to attain given objectives in per capita output) operate in sparsely settled as well as in densely settled countries. In very sparsely settled countries the adverse effect upon the possible reduction of density relative to capital of rapid growth of the labor force may be partially offset by an increasingly advantageous relationship between numbers and land area and other resources. A larger population may, when original density is unusually low, permit the use of more efficient large-scale operations. This possibility does not imply, however, that the more rapid the rate of growth the better. Additional capital for the additional labor force is still essential, and rapid growth prevents an increase in the capital/worker rates. Moreover, from a strictly economic point of view the most advantageous way to attain a larger labor force is through immigration, because it is possible by this means to obtain additional labor without incurring the expense of childhood dependency.

Declining fertility and per capita income: Summary

A reduction in fertility has the immediate effect (during the first generation after the decline begins) of reducing the burden of child dependency without any major effect on the size of the labor force. After twenty or twenty-five years the decline in fertility begins to effect a major reduction in the rate of growth of the labor force. In the more remote future, beginning after forty or fifty years and with increasing importance with the further passage of time, reduced fertility produces a population of lower density—with a smaller labor force relative to the available resources. The age distribution effect of reduced fertility operates to produce during the first generation a larger total national product than would result if fertility had not been reduced. The greater rise in total output results from the fact that the same number of producers— the same number of persons eligible for participation in the labor force —is accompanied by a smaller number of consumers. The smaller number of consumers decreases the fraction of national output that must be allocated to current consumption, and thus promotes the mobilization of resources for economic growth. Both private savings and the ability of the government to raise funds for development are increased.

In addition, a smaller number of consumers (especially children) permits the expenditure of savings and tax receipts in ways that raise national output more (or more immediately) than other uses. Less must be spent for primary education, housing and "social overhead" purposes generally.

Another indirect effect of reduced fertility is that, as a result of larger per capita consumption, the labor force is perhaps more productive because of better nutrition, and because of the effects of rising consumption in combatting apathy, and in providing better work incentives. These effects of a reduced number of consumers relative to the producers in the population caused in the short run by a decline in fertility continue into the future so long as fertility remains below its former level. Starting after twenty-five or thirty years is the additional effect of reduced fertility in slowing down the growth of the labor force. A reduced rate of growth of the labor force means that a given level of net investment can be used to add more to the per capita endowment of the labor force in productive equipment than if the labor force were growing more rapidly.

In the long run the slower rate of growth that reduced fertility brings would result in much lower density of population than with the continuation of high fertility. Even with a fifty per cent reduction in fertility, the population in most underdeveloped areas would grow very substantially during the next two or three generations. For example, in the projection presented earlier showing typical prospects for Latin American countries, with fertility falling by one half, density would be multiplied by 2.46 in thirty years and by 1.71 in the ensuing thirty years, a total increase of 4.2 times in sixty years. In spite of greatly reduced fertility, the density of workers relative to resources would increase by a factor of something like four in the next two generations.

Brazil is often cited as a country that might derive economic benefits from more dense settlement. Even with a fifty per cent reduction in fertility, the population of Brazil aged fifteen to sixty-four will have increased from 38 million to 161 million in the next sixty years. This would give Brazil a population at these ages sixty years from now forty-two per cent larger than that of the United States today. It is hard to argue that this density would be too small to achieve an efficient exploitation of Brazil's resources, especially since much of Brazil's vast area is of uncertain economic value. Not all underdeveloped areas have as high a current growth potential as Latin America. Current fertility is in many instances below that found in Mexico or Brazil, and in other instances success in reducing mortality is somewhat behind the achievements of the more advanced Latin American countries. In India, for example, where current fertility is probably lower than that of Mexico, Brazil, or Colombia and current mortality higher, the increase in the labor force in the next two generations, if fertility were to be cut in half in the next twenty-five years, would be only two and a half to three times rather than more than four times. It should be added that any increases in density are scarcely advantageous to India's economy.

In sum, the population density that would result from a fifty per cent reduction in fertility in the next twenty-five years would in almost every underdeveloped area be at least adequate for the efficient exploitation of the resources available. The much *higher* density that would result from sustained fertility, a margin of higher density that would increase with ever greater rapidity the further into the future one looks, might in the most favorable circumstances cause no insuperable difficulties for a few decades. It might be possible, for example, to offset a high density of population in some areas, as Hong Kong has done, by engaging in trade, provided there remain areas of the world prepared to supply agricultural products and raw materials in exchange for finished goods and services. But in all areas, a prolonged continuation of rapid growth would lead to intolerable overcrowding.

Gains in income per head

It is possible to estimate roughly the cumulative advantage that reduced fertility brings in the form of more rapidly increasing income per head. Such calculations have been made at the Office of Population Research utilizing alternative population projections and concomitant economic projections based on the demographic and economic data of two countries, India and Mexico. In each instance we assumed that increases in savings per consumer were proportional to increases in income per consumer. In calculating the number of "consumers" each child under fifteen was counted as only one half. Thus the calculations make a conservative allowance for the effect of the burden of childhood dependency. These calculations take account of the estimates of government authorities and economists in each country with regard to such matters as the expected productivity of new investments and of the allocation of funds to education, housing, and other social overhead categories. On the basis of precisely equivalent assumptions about the determination of the future growth of national output, national output was projected into the future, in conjunction with two alternative population projections. These alternative population projections were analogous to the illustrative projections that have served as the basis of our discussion here. The contrasting projections for each country assumed a continuation of past trends of declining mortality, and assumed two alternative future courses of fertility: unchanged on the one hand, and reduced in a linear fashion by fifty per cent in twenty-five years on the other.

In spite of different initial economic and demographic conditions—Mexico has higher fertility and lower mortality than India, a substantially higher initial per capita income, and is further advanced in most aspects of industrialization and modernization, having for example a relatively larger manufacturing sector and a relatively smaller agricultural sector in the economy—the estimated proportionate gains resulting from reduced fertility were almost identical in the two countries. Table 2 shows the ratio of income per consumer with reduced fertility to income per consumer for sustained fertility at various dates following the initiation of the fertility decline. The difference is small at first but amounts to forty per cent after thirty years and more than one hundred per cent in sixty years. After 150 years the low fertility population would have an income per consumer six times as high as the faster growing population with unchanged fertility.

These calculations make no allowance for any adverse effects caused by high density. They allow only for the effect of differences in age distribution and of different rates of growth in the labor force. These projections of the advantages of reduced fertility implicitly assume a world of unlimted resources, and thereby understate the gains a lower birth rate would bring.

TABLE 2

Income per equivalent adult consumer in Projection B (fertility reduced), income per consumer with sustained fertility = 100

Income per consumer in Projection B, income per consumer in A = 100
Time in years

0	10	20	30	40	50	60	70	80	90	100	...	150
100	103	114	141	163	186	209	235	264	297	334	...	596

Delaying reduction in fertility

There is a persuasive *laissez-faire* position on population policy in the pre-industrial countries, based on the following argument. Every country that has become highly industrialized has experienced a decline in fertility amounting to at least fifty per cent of the pre-industrial level. Therefore, the argument runs, public policy should be concentrated on achieving the maximum pace of industrialization. The decline in fertility will take care of itself.

The generalization upon which this argument rests is well founded. All countries that have become predominantly urban, that have shifted away from agriculture as the source of employment for as much as half of the labor force, and that now have adult populations that are at least eighty-five per cent literate have experienced at least a fifty per cent decline in fertility. Included among these countries are: all of Europe (except for Albania); the overseas industrialized countries with predominantly European populations—Australia, New Zealand, Canada and the United States; Japan and the Soviet Union. However, it is far from clear precisely what aspects of industrialization have been instrumental in causing the decline in fertility in these countries. In some instances industrialization had preceded for a long time and had effected major changes in the economy and society before any tangible reduction in fertility occurred. For example, a marked decline did not begin in England and Wales until the 1880's, nor in Japan until about 1925. For countries that are as yet in the early stages of modernization, having very low current per capita incomes, it might take at least thirty to sixty years to attain a state of industrialization that would in itself cause a rapid decline in fertility. In fact the adverse effects of continued high fertility in the interim might in itself postpone the attainment of the needed state of advanced industrialization. Table 3 shows the ratio of

TABLE 3

Income per equivalent adult consumer, with immediately reduced fertility, income per consumer with fertility reduced after 30 years = 100

Income per consumer in Projection B, income in projection with delayed decline in fertility = 100

Time in years

0	10	20	30	40	50	60	70	80	90	100	...	150
100	103	114	141	158	163	149	144	141	141	141	...	141

income per consumer in a population where a fifty per cent decline in fertility spread over twenty-five years begins immediately to output per consumer in a population where fertility remains unchanged for thirty years and then begins a fifty per cent reduction in twenty-five years. Note that the advantage of the early reduction in fertility reaches a maximum in about fifty years and then settles back to a permanent advantage of about forty per cent (the gain previously noted at the end of thirty years from a decline in fertility).

The calculation underlying this table was based on the assumption that the relative advantage to be gained by fertility reduction shown in Table 2 would apply no matter when the reduction began. Again as in Table 2 itself no allowance is made for the adverse effects of higher density. The long-run population resulting from a reduction in fertility postponed by thirty years would be sixty-four per cent larger than the population arising from an immediate reduction in fertility. Table 3 makes no allowance for the possibility that a population sixty-four per cent bigger would because of greater density tend to have lower per capita output.

In sum, the advantages of an early reduction in fertility shown in Table 3 are a minimum estimate. To wait for an automatic decline in fertility (if a program of family planning could cause an earlier reduction) is to forego *at least* the relative gains in income per consumer shown in this table. Any allowance for the deleterious effects of greater density would serve to increase the estimated cost of postponement. There is moreover the possibility that the slower progress of industrialization with sustained fertility, especially when great increases in an already high density are involved, might postpone the expected attainment of an "automatic" fertility decline.

POPULATION AND THE LABOR FORCE

It is of course a drastic oversimplification to treat industrialization and modernization wholly in terms of increases in income per head. Such increases are surely a valid and necessary objective of economic development, but there are other goals widely shared in the underdeveloped areas, including better health and improved and more widespread education, rightly viewed as values in themselves, as well as means of achieving larger incomes. A nearly universal goal is that of providing productive employment for male adults and for a proportion of adult women that steadily increases as modernization proceeds. This goal, like those of better health and education, is considered as valuable in its own right, because of the degrading effect of unemployment or of unproductive employment.

The problems of "unemployment" and "underemployment," which are the subject of so much comment in the underdeveloped areas, are essentially reflections of the poverty and low productivity to which these areas are subject. Underemployment is sometimes defined as a situation in which a reduction in the number of persons engaged in a given activity would not cause an important reduction in total output from the activity in question. Examples are the presence of more porters in a railway station than are needed to carry the normal load of luggage, farming operations where a traditional set of tasks are divided among whatever family members have the responsibility for operating the farm, or a cluster of small retail shops carrying essentially identical merchandise in which the clerks or proprietors are idle most of the day because of the scarcity of customers. In most underdeveloped areas such examples are common. The existence of essentially redundant manpower that these examples indicate is called "underemployment" rather than "unemployment" because the redundancy does not show itself in the form of large numbers actively looking for work. The measurement of unemployment (and the technical defintion of unemployment) has become increasingly a matter of determining the number of persons actively seeking jobs. In most underdeveloped areas a major increase in the number of productive jobs would be needed to make serious inroads into current underemployment and unemployment. The prospective rapid growth in the labor force that such countries face adds greatly to the difficulties of achieving satisfactory employment goals. During the first generation the number of additional productive jobs that must be provided is scarcely affected by the course of fertility. The labor force thirty years following the start of a fifty per cent reduction in fertility spread evenly over a twenty-five year period is less than ten per cent smaller than the labor force resulting from a continuation of unchanged fertility. In a typical Latin American population the labor force would increase in thirty years by a factor of 2.44 should fertility be reduced, and 2.67 should fertility remain unchanged. In either case the provision of adequate employment opportunities is a job of frightening proportions. An annual increase of about three per cent or more in the number of jobs is required if unemployment and underemployment are not to increase.

In underdeveloped areas the barrier to more adequate employment opportunity is not primarily that lack of sufficient effective demand which many economists see as the source of the apparently chronic problem of attaining full employment in the United States. The simultaneous existence of unemployed persons and idle capital equipment in the United States (a conspicuous example is the steel industry) is not the situation typical of the underdeveloped countries. The absence of opportunities for productive employment is primarily the result of insufficient productive equipment and resources for labor to work with, compounded by the lack of education and training on the part of the labor force itself.

In the earlier discussion it was seen that a population with reduced fertility has important advantages in its capacity to accumulate capital. It also can more readily provide a rapid attainment of specified educational standards. Consequently, even during the first twenty-five or thirty years following the start of fertility decline, when the number of new jobs needed each year is not much affected by reduced fertility, the advantages in reduced dependency that lower fertility brings would, by enabling higher levels of investment, permit the more rapid expansion of employment opportunity. In the longer run the reduced rate of growth of the labor force resulting from lower fertility would make the achievement of adequate employment opportunities much easier. After sixty years, for example, the rate of increase in the labor force in our model projection for a Latin American country would be 3.7 per cent if fertility were sustained, and only 1.3 per cent if fertility were reduced. By that time the number of persons sixteen to sixty-four in the lower fertility projection would be nearly 4.2 times as great as today, and with sustained fertility it would be eight times as great.

The magnitude of the problem of providing future jobs in the underdeveloped countries can be better appreciated when one considers the typical change in the composition of employment that accompanies the process of industrialization. In general terms the change in patterns of employment is one of increasing diversity, with reduced proportions in the traditional occupations, especially in agriculture. If the employment history in the industrialized countries is examined, the universal trend during the process of industrialization is found to be a steadily decreasing proportion in agriculture. In fact all of the more highly industrialized countries have reached or passed through a phase in which the *number* in agriculture remains constant, so that all of the increases in the population of labor force age are absorbed in the non-agricultural sectors of the economy. This phase has then typically been followed by a decline in the absolute number of persons dependent on agriculture. It is not surprising that such a decline has been experienced in countries such as England and Wales, known for their emphasis on manufacturing and for their exports of manufactured products and imports of agricultural products. It is somewhat unexpected that a decline should have occurred in Denmark, a major exporter of agricultural produce. Decreases in the absolute number in agriculture have also been recorded in countries of very different densities, ranging from England and Japan on the one hand to the United States, the Soviet Union, and New Zealand on the other.

At some stage, then, an industrializing country must, if it follows the sequence common to the history of the now industrialized countries, look to the non-agricultural sector of the economy for the provision of employment opportunities sufficient for the whole increase in the labor force. Table 4 shows the magnitude of this goal with two model population projections and three illustrative different starting points in terms of the proportion of the labor force now engaged in agriculture. In most underdeveloped countries it will be impossible to achieve these rates of increase in non-agricultural employment. They will be forced to continue to increase the number of persons engaged in agriculture. Such continued increases are at best a necessary evil. In fact these unavoidable increases in agricultural employment show the cost of an initial high level of density in a country that has a high proportion of its labor force engaged in agriculture. Such countries cannot provide non-agricultural employment opportunities for the whole of the increase in their labor forces, and because of the small land holdings that high density implies, additions to the labor force in agriculture add mostly to underemployment in this sector.

It is a reasonable, almost an essential objective that within a generation most countries should plan to provide non-agricultural employment for the whole of their additions to the labor force. Table 4 shows how greatly eased is the task if fertility is reduced rather than allowed to remain at current high levels.

This sketchy analysis is sufficient to show that the reduction of fertility would play an even more crucial role in attaining the goal of

TABLE 4

Average annual per cent increase in non-agricultural employment required if all of the increased labor force is to be employed outside agriculture

Required annual per cent increase in employment
Period

Per cent in agriculture at t = 0	Projection	0-10 years	10-20 years	20-30 years	30-40 years	40-50 years	50-60 years
70	A	7.3	5.9	5.1	4.6	4.4	4.2
	B	7.3	5.7	4.0	2.7	2.2	1.9
60	A	6.2	5.3	4.8	4.4	4.3	4.1
	B	6.2	5.1	3.8	2.6	2.1	1.8
50	A	5.3	4.8	4.5	4.3	4.2	4.0
	B	5.3	4.7	3.5	2.5	2.0	1.8

adequate employment opportunities than in the closely related but not identical goal of insuring a more rapid increase in income per consumer.

SUMMARY

The underdeveloped areas in the world for the next fifty years or so have a choice at best between very rapid growth and moderately rapid growth in population. Any low-income country that succeeds in initiating an immediate reduction in fertility would in the short run enjoy a reduction in the burden of child dependency that would permit a higher level of investment and more immediately productive uses of investment.

After twenty-five or thirty years the advantage of reduced dependency would be enhanced by a markedly slower growth of the labor force, making it possible to achieve a faster growth in capital per worker from any given investment, and making it easier to approach the goal of productive employment for all who need it.

In the long run, the slower rate of growth that fertility reduction causes would reduce the overwhelming multiplication of density that continued rapid growth implies.

The additional gains in per capita income resulting from a fifty per cent reduction in fertility occurring within twenty-five years would be about forty per cent in thirty years, 100 per cent in sixty years, and 500 per cent in 150 years, neglecting the effects of density. To postpone the reduction by thirty years is to add sixty-four per cent to the size of the population in the long run, and to suffer a loss in potential long-range gains from the interim reduction in dependency of forty per cent. In sum, a reduction in fertility would make the process of modernization more rapid and more certain. It would accelerate the growth in income, provide more rapidly the possibility of productive employment for all adults who need jobs, make the attainment of universal education easier —and it would have the obvious and immediate effect of providing the women of low-income countries some relief from constant pregnancy, parturition and infant care.

Donald J. Bogue

5

Population Growth in the United States

When the topic of overpopulation is introduced, one often gets the impression that Americans tend to heave a sigh of relief that here, at least, is one thing about which we need not worry. Uncle Sam is paying farmers not to grow food. Billions of dollars of food surpluses are stored in little crib cities throughout the agricultural regions. Although it is true that starvation from overpopulation is a remote possibility here, whereas it is an emergent reality in other parts of the world, the United States has its population problems too. Our lives may not be at stake, but our way of life and standard of living are imperiled. Just as over-rapid population growth threatens to eat up the social and economic gains for which the nations of Asia, Africa and Latin America are working, so it threatens to devour many of the social and economic gains which the United States has gained, and to which it still aspires. Here and in other economically advanced nations, therefore, rapid population growth is a threat less to subsistence than to living. Since 1946 our rate of population growth has been so high as to lead some experts to call it, also, a "population explosion."

Such growth has a high social and economic cost, which merits full consideration. We have not yet become fully aware of our increased growth since 1946. Some of the more serious effects will begin to be felt quite strongly by 1965, for after this date the population count will

DONALD J. BOGUE *is Director of the Community and Family Study Center and Associate Director of the Population Research and Training Center at the University of Chicago. He serves as consultant to the U. S. Bureau of the Census, to the National Center for Health Statistics of the Public Health Service, and to the Division of Statistical Standards of the Bureau of the Budget. He is President-elect of the Population Association of America (1962-63) and a Fellow of the American Statistical Association. His publications include* The Population of the United States *and* Economic Areas of the United States.

mount higher and higher in amounts that will make the building of sub-divisions in one year to provide housing for the growth of a half-dozen average-sized metropolitan areas the equivalent of the entire settlement of the West.

These are strong assertions. Let us examine the facts of present and prospective growth on which they are based, and then search for their implications.

CURRENT AND PROSPECTIVE GROWTH

The population of the United States is the fourth largest in the world. Only China, India and the USSR have larger populations. On July 1, 1963, we numbered about 190 million persons, which is one six-teenth of all of the earth's population. Thus we comprise only a com-paratively small proportion of the earth's human creatures. But in pro-portion to land area, we have our share (the United States land area is about six per cent of the earth's total land).

Our population is now increasing at the rate of three million per-sons per year. Never before in the nation's history has the population growth been so great as in recent years. Our actual growth of thirty million from April 1953 to April 1963 was equal to the entire net growth of the territory which is now the United States during the two and a third centuries from the landing of the pilgrims to the Civil War (1620 to 1860). It is equal to nearly twice the growth of the nation during any decade since the nation was established.

Despite this tremendous volume of growth, the *rate* of growth ex-pressed in percentage terms does not seem impressively high. It is only 1.63 per cent per year (for 1960-61). Among the nations of the world this is about an average rate of growth, or even a little below average. Most of the nations of Europe are growing more slowly than this, while most of Asia and Latin America are growing more rapidly. In Europe, a growth rate of 0.5 to 0.75 per cent is about average, while in Asia and Latin America the average growth rate is about 2.5 per cent per year. But 1.63 per cent of 190 million is equal to 3.1 million persons.

The fact that the population is able to grow by such large amounts with what appears to be only a small rate has a very important implica-tion: as the population size increases, if the rate remains the same, the amount of annual increase will become larger and larger. The annual increments ultimately become so large that numbers which look impos-sibly high are obtained. For example, if our current population of 190 million persons continues to grow for only one century at its present rate, the population of the United States would be about one billion persons. This is equivalent to one-third of the world's present inhabitants, and would be roughly equivalent to moving all of the population of Europe,

TABLE I

Projected Population for the United States at Each Census, 1970 to 2060, on the Assumption that the Population Continues to Grow at the Rate of 1.63 Per Cent Per Year and at the Rate of 0.8 Per Cent Per Year

Year	Assume annual rate is 1.63		Assume annual rate is 0.8	
	Estimated population (millions)	Estimated increase during preceding decade (millions)	Estimated population (millions)	Estimated increase during preceding decade (millions)
1960..........	180	28	180	28
1970..........	212	32	195	15
1980..........	249	37	211	16
1990..........	292	43	229	18
2000..........	344	51	248	19
2010..........	404	61	268	20
2020..........	475	71	290	22
2030..........	558	83	314	24
2040..........	656	98	341	27
2050..........	771	115	369	28
2060..........	907	137	399	30
2065..........	1,000	...	416	...

Latin America and Africa into the territory of the fifty states. Table 1 reports what the population of the United States would be at each census for the next century if it continues to grow at the rate of 1960-61; Figure 1 charts the trend population growth would take.

During the depth of the economic depression, the growth rate sank to a record low of 0.8 per cent for the year 1933. The population has never grown more slowly than this in the nation's history. If we returned to this level instantaneously, we would still have a very large population by 2065, as Table 1 shows. Projecting the curve for only a few decades beyond one hundred years leads to numbers which quickly become fantastically high, even at the slow rate of growth.

What does this mean for America? It means that although we are not yet aware we have a population problem, we nevertheless have all the ingredients of a very serious one which could reach very critical proportions in only a generation from now. If present rates continue, our children born today, if they live to retire at age sixty-five, will be living in a nation nearly *three times* as populous as at present. Thus, the intolerable impact of run-away population growth is not a spectre that can

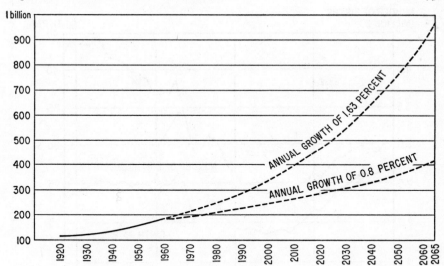

Figure 1. Projected growth of U. S. population on the assumption that it continues to grow (A) at the 1961-62 rate of 1.63 per cent per year and (B) at the minimal rate of 0.8 per cent per year.

be banished to far-away places like India and China. It is lurking in the background here, and could blight the lives of our children and grandchildren already born or to be born from now on.

These calculations are straightforward and simple. They are based on an expected birth rate of 23.6 per thousand population and a death rate of 9.3 and a very limited amount of immigration. Applying the annual rate of 1.63 to the 1960 population, using the compound interest formula, yields the results just cited. The picture is rendered even more dismal by the realization that the population of almost every nation on earth outside Europe is racing toward a level that is of even greater magnitude than that of the United States (see Chapters 2 and 3).

The boom babies grow up

The prolonged "baby boom" of 1946-1963 emerged as a surprise to most demographers after the low and falling birth rates during the 1930's (see Figure 2). During the period 1926 to 1941, in fact, the number of births actually fell below those of earlier years, and the nation seemed headed toward a leveling off in total population size, and perhaps even a decline.

If Figure 2 is studied carefully, the nature of the problem becomes clearer.

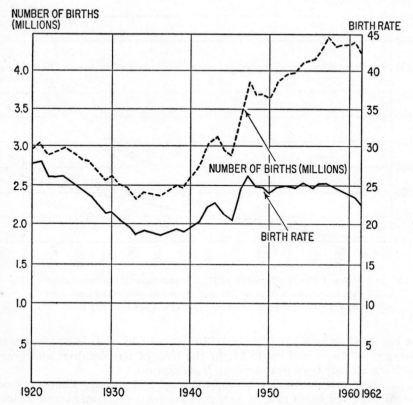

Figure 2. Trend in the number of live births and in the crude birth rate, 1920 to 1962.

1. From 1920 to 1933 the birth *rate* fell steadily and by a substantial number of points. It declined from 27.7 in 1920 to 18.4 in 1933 (a decline of 35 per cent). Meanwhile, the annual *number* of births declined much more slowly. There was no decline at all to speak of until 1926-27, but the rate fell so sharply after 1926 that the number of births declined. But the decline in birth numbers was much less than in the birth rate. This happened because the declining rate was applied to a base of women of childbearing age that was still growing.

2. When the birth rate rose in the 1940's, there was a very substantial increase in the annual number of births. Between 1946 and 1951 the *increase* amounted to more than one million births per year. During these five years the moderately high rate of about twenty-five per thousand was applied to the rather large group of women born during the years 1916 to 1924, when the birth rate was also moderately high—about twenty-seven per thousand.

3. Figure 2 shows that the onset of the baby boom came just as the first of the smaller cohorts born between 1925 and 1945 (idem) grew up, married, and began to produce children. *Since 1945 our corps of child-bearers has been comprised of a shrinking number of women of prime childbearing age.* As of 1963, the last of the undersized cohorts had entered the reproductive age, and hereafter the number of women of childbearing age will increase rapidly. From now on birth rates must fall by a substantial amount just to keep the number of births constant at about four and one-half million.

But what has happened to the birth rate in the last few years? Figure 2 shows that since 1957 it has been declining steadily. But we must remember that this is the *crude* birth rate (births per 1,000 population), and includes in the denominator the large and increasing number of children born since 1946. A more refined way of measuring the fertility rate is to observe the rate for each age group and then to compute an age-standardized general fertility rate based upon women of childbearing age only. Demographers are generally agreed that this is the best single measure of fertility level.

Table 2 reports the age specific fertility rate of the United States population for 1950 and 1960, and the age standardized general fertility rates—with per cent change in the measures. The data are reported separately for the white and nonwhite population in order that we may

TABLE 2

Age Specific Fertility Rates and Summary Rates of Fertility for the White and Nonwhite Populations of the United States: 1950 to 1960

Fertility measures	White			Nonwhite		
	1960	1950	Per cent change 1950-1960	1960	1950	Per cent change 1950-1960
Age Specific Rates						
15-19 years	79.8	70.3	+13.5	163.4	169.0	−3.4
20-24 years	252.8	190.4	+32.8	294.2	242.6	+21.3
25-29 years	194.9	165.1	+18.0	214.6	173.8	+23.5
30-34 years	109.6	102.6	+6.8	135.6	112.6	+20.4
35-39 years	54.0	51.4	+5.1	74.2	64.3	+15.4
40-44 years	14.7	14.5	+1.4	22.0	21.2	+3.8
45-49 years	0.8	1.0	−20.0	1.7	2.6	−52.9
Summary Rates						
Crude birth rate	22.7	23.0	−1.3	32.1	33.3	−3.7
General fertility rate (births per 1,000 women 15-44)	113.2	102.3	+10.7	153.6	137.3	+11.9
Standardized fertility rate	105.8	89.2	+18.8	139.7	120.9	+15.6
Total fertility rate (15-44)	3,533	2,976	+18.7	4,528	3,929	+15.2

make comparisons later. From this table emerges a most surprising finding: American fertility *increased* sharply between 1950 and 1960, despite the fact that the crude birth rates were falling. For the white population the standardized general fertility rate rose from 84.2 to 109.5, an increase of twenty-three per cent. For the nonwhite population, it increased by fifteen per cent. The table shows that the greatest increases occurred in the age group 20-29 for whites and 20-34 for nonwhites.

The explanation for this apparent contradiction lies, of course, in the smaller number of women available for childbearing between 1950 and 1960. The "baby boom" was created by an unusually small cohort of women of childbearing age who have been bearing children at a rapid rate, a rate that has been rising.

Lay observers have been noting the fall in the *crude* birth rate and are beginning to conclude that the "baby boom" is over. This is a great oversimplification and may be far from the truth. Instead, we possibly are facing a sudden spurt in population growth that could make the baby boom of 1946 look small. In fact, the only way it can be averted is for birth rates for women of all ages to decline by fifteen to twenty-five per cent.

The reason for this is that we are moving into an era when the number of women of childbearing age will be increasing rapidly. The following table gives the picture. The number of women of childbearing age (fifteen to forty-four years of age) at each census 1930-60, and the projected number to 1990, is as follows:

Year	Number of Women 15-44 (millions)	Number of Women 20-29 (millions)
1930	29	11
1940	32	12
1950	34	12
1960	36	11
1970	43	15
1980	54	20
1990	70	22

These are actual population counts or official population projections of the U. S. Bureau of Census, and there is very little guess work in them. For all but an insignificant portion of the population of 1980, they represent persons who were already born in 1960, and who will be merely growing up to enter the reproductive ages. A look at these figures shows how the number of women of childbearing ages (and especially in the peak years of childbearing, 20-29) has remained nearly constant for the past twenty to thirty years, but how it will undergo a phenomenal increase during the present decade. No matter what the birth rates are during the next two decades, they will apply to a population of childbearers that will double between 1960 and 1990. It will take a most dramatic fall in birth rates to avoid extremely rapid population growth in the next twenty years. It *is* possible for this decrease to occur. The American population knows how to use contraception effectively if it so desires. There is some evidence that as of 1962 it was beginning to take some action to reduce the fertility rates. The big question is, "Will the reduction be big enough and fast enough to avert serious social and economic dislocation?"

A careful study of the incomplete statistics at hand suggests that *perhaps* in 1961 or 1962 there was a *start* toward reduction in fertility. Applying the age-specific fertility rates of 1960 to the number of women of childbearing age estimated for 1962 yields an estimate of the number of births expected in 1962 if there had been no change in fertility levels. Extrapolating the preliminary data for January to October of 1962 population (the last month for which data are available), it appears that the 1962 population failed to achieve this expected amount by 2.5 per cent. In other words, when the factors of age and race are held constant, the American birth rate seems to have declined by 2.5 per cent in the last two years. This may very well be the beginning of a major readjustment to demographic reality. But so far the extent of this curtailment is much too small to offset the very great impact of the increased number of childbearers who will replace the small cohorts of depression childbearers just now passing out of the picture. At least one-half of the recent decline in the crude birth rate is due to the rapidly changing age composition of the childbearing force of women. Thus, as the baby boom babies grow up, they threaten to initiate another round of population growth, simply because the number of childbearers will be greatly increased. They will also have other effects, which we will now examine.

THE NEXT 25 YEARS

America's population problem has more dimensions than that which relates to the attempt to reduce fertility under conditions of a rising number of childbearers. Even if we could by some magical trick lower fertility today to a point where it would level off and not rise above 4.5 million births per year, we would still be faced with population problems of a thorny nature. In 1963 there was an unprecedented number of infants and children up to seventeen years old, born after the onset of the baby boom in 1946. These children have caused some inconvenience and public concern because of the demands they have made upon the economy. We have had to build grammar schools at a pace so rapid that only federal intervention has managed to prevent a catastrophe in many communities. Even so, double-shift classes have become commonplace, and teachers have been burdened with oversize classes. There have been other inconveniences: the station wagon has become stylish; the much more expensive four-bedroom house or apartment has come into demand again after a quarter-century of declining popularity. Juvenile delinquency has been on the increase in badly overcrowded slum areas; television and other mass media have been accused of catering to the tremendous juvenile audience rather than to the much smaller adult audience.

But these changes and inconveniences are probably minor in comparison with those in store in the next 25 years. Beginning in June 1964, and in every June thereafter, our high schools will spew out a graduating class of students that will be, on the average, one million students larger than the previous level. For each three graduates in 1960 there will be four graduates after 1965.

The current flurry over "school drop-outs" is just an out-of-focus example of the forthcoming problem. The *rate* of school drop-outs has *not* risen. In fact, it has declined. But the number of children now in the upper grades who are exposed to the possibility of dropping out has increased so much that a new and serious problem has been created. During the quarter century 1965 to 1990 a whole series of population problems of this type will unfold. The foundations for each one have already been laid, because the actors have already joined the cast and are only awaiting their cue to enter on stage at the appropriate moment of the life cycle. We will discuss some of these problems.

High school enrollment

The baby boom cohorts are just now beginning to have their impact upon the high schools. By January 1, 1965, the entire high school system will consist of baby boom enrollees. Thereafter, the high school enrollment will continue to rise at a steady rate of about three per cent per year until 1980, as babies already born grow up to enter high school. Projections prepared by the Bureau of Census indicate an expected enrollment of 15.1 million students in high schools in 1970 in comparison with 10.1 in 1960. In the decade 1960-70, the enrollment in grammar school will remain about stationary, while high school enrollment will jump by fifty per cent.

What happens to the high school enrollment after 1980 depends, of course, upon the course of the birth rate after 1960-62. We might add, parenthetically, that the peak of the expansion in grammar school enrollment seems to have been reached. During the years 1963 to 1970 it will remain stationary. This is due to the fact that the number of births has remained comparatively steady for the past eight to ten years.

The cost of providing education at the high school level is greater per pupil-year, because of the much greater number, variety and complexity of the facilities required. For this reason, public reaction to the rising expenditures for secondary public schools may be much stronger than for elementary schools. Unless facilities are provided, the quality of training given can fall precipitously.

College enrollment

The college enrollment picture is similar to that for high schools except that it is complicated by two additional factors:

(a) the rapidly rising rate of college attendance, as an increasing proportion of students leaving high school go on to college; and

(b) the prolongation of college education with a growing emphasis upon post-graduate training.

Projections of the college enrollment have been made to 1980 by the United States Bureau of Census. A near doubling of college enrollments is forecast for the decade 1960-70 and a fifty per cent increase for the decade 1970-80. From the calculations made it appears that within the twenty years from 1960 to 1980 college and professional enrollment will treble in size. The estimated college enrollment by years is as follows:

Year	Millions of Students
1960	4
1965	6
1970	8
1975	10
1980	12

A few of the very first of the baby boom babies enrolled as college freshmen in the autumn of 1962. This trickle is destined to become a flood, so that by 1965 the enrollment will be about 1.7 million above the four million of 1960. Since college and especially graduate training require far more elaborate and costly facilities than high school, it is clear that the task of educating the children of the baby boom at a high level will be most expensive. The problem of maintaining quality in teaching and standards of excellence in student performance under these conditions may be very serious in the next two decades.

The exploding labor market

The same enlarged cohorts of young persons who will be invading colleges will also be seeking jobs. Consequently, the labor force is beginning to experience an explosion of growth at the present time, and will continue to do so for at least the next twenty-five years. This expansion has already begun because many of the boom babies have already passed the minimum fourteen-year age limit, and have begun to work instead of continuing in school. The following table, prepared from projections of the United States Census Bureau, shows what future employment levels will probably be like:

Year	Labor force (millions)	Increase per Year (millions)
1960	73	1.0
1965	79	1.2
1970	87	1.5
1975	94	1.4
1980	100	1.3

We are currently adding a net of more than one million new workers each year. By 1970 this will have been stepped up to a 1.5 million increase in workers per year. Such expansion will result, by 1980, in a labor force of about one hundred million persons. This estimate is very likely to materialize, because all but an insignificant fraction of the workers-to-be have already been born; the process of maturation will bring them into the labor force, barring a national calamity or war. The trend of labor force participation rates is also relatively stable and reasonably predictable. Never in its history has the nation been faced with such an expansion in the work force. Labor is a commodity which must go to market as it is produced by the nation's school systems. What effect such a large supply will have upon wages or prices is not clear. It remains to be seen whether the economy can absorb new workers at this rate without gradually building up a large volume of hard core unemployment. Some economists see labor force expansion as an important spur to the economy, because these young workers will bring with them a vast demand for additional production—automobiles, houses, and all of the purchases that accompany the establishment of a new household.

A point which needs to be considered is that with an expanded labor market it will be possible to develop a large caste of unemployed persons under the guise of "business normality." Even if unemployment levels of five to seven per cent remain in effect, by 1980 this will mean a total of five to seven million unemployed on a routine basis. This represents a total *volume* of human misery on a *routine basis* more than half as great as was experienced during the great economic depression of 1931-40. A really severe recession could send the number of unemployed skyrocketing to over fifteen million. The potentialities for the quantity of human suffering that can now emanate from even moderate business recessions are becoming immense.

There is evidence already that this problem is beginning to plague us, and create a drag on our economic progress. Until recently, urban poverty in the United States has had almost a hundred per cent turnover from generation to generation; the children of the poor in one generation almost all climbed into the middle income bracket and were replaced by a fresh wave of in-migrants from rural areas. Now there is mounting evidence that this process is slowing down, so that in our slums the poor are begetting children destined to remain poor. We are hearing more and more of families and individuals on relief whose parents also were on relief, and of the emergence of a "culture of dependency." The recent book, *National Income and Welfare* by Morgen, David, *et al.*, provides statistical evidence that this actually is occurring, and is not just a nightmare conjured up by sociologists. That Negro citizens are being singled out to comprise this caste of professional public dependents makes it an even more worrisome population problem.

Future households

An average household at the present time contains 3.4 persons. It is clear that there will be a vast increase in the number of households—roughly one million per year from 1965 to 1975 and even greater thereafter. This is roughly equivalent to building one complete Chicago during each year in the foreseeable future merely to keep abreast of population growth—without replacing housing already built.

A very large quantity of housing built in the 1920's and earlier is becoming obsolete and in need of replacement. By 1980 much of this will have become substandard. In order to clear and replace it a large program of renewal will be required. Whether this can be done at a time when such vast amounts of housing are needed merely to keep abreast of population growth will depend upon the level of prosperity and purchasing power of the population. If the labor force succeeds in absorbing the new cohorts as they emerge, the housing needed may be produced as a simple matter of keeping up with the market. If, however, purchasing power lags, there may be a serious housing problem.

In 1958 the U. S. Bureau of Census prepared projections of future trends in the number of households; and these are still reasonably precise estimations of what we may expect. The census in 1960 counted 53.0 million households instead of the 51.9 million households projected, but the *trends* envisaged would be roughly the same. The following table summarizes these trends:

Year	Increase in Households during the Year (000)
1960	701
1961	482
1962	730
1963	857
1964	878
1965	750
1966	776
1967	867
1968	1,019
1969	830
1970	886

It is clear that under almost any set of assumptions, the nation is faced with the need for a major house-building program to handle its population growth.

Future expenditures for community facilities

Within the next two decades, population growth will require a substantial extension of community facilities. Despite the fact that they have constructed numerous, costly and elaborate freeways, a majority of metropolitan areas have serious traffic problems that can be solved only by additional public outlays for more freeways, or by the construction of subway systems. The problem of water supply is becoming extremely serious in many metropolitan areas, and one that can be solved only by the construction of new systems that tap new supplies—often hundreds of miles away. Population growth has caused the flow of sewage to mount to such proportions that not only is its disposal a problem, but it also complicates greatly the problem of water supply elsewhere. High densities of great populations are bringing problems of smog and air pollution. As our population grows, present parks and other recreation facilities are becoming badly overloaded, and the taxpayer is asked to approve bond issues for acquisition of new areas, in addition to the bonds for subways, water purification systems, sewage disposal systems, etc.

Many economists would maintain that each new unit of population brings with it the added earning power (and hence tax-paying power) to repay the community for the added facilities it must build. Others point out that cities, increasing in size and complexity, eventually reach a point where additional units have a more-than-proportional cost, and that the modern metropolis is reaching or has reached this point. In the future, population growth may impose costly financial burdens which fiscally weakened municipalities will be ill prepared to bear.

Irrespective of which of these two views is correct, the next three decades are going to require extensive expansion in community facilities, and the funds for providing them must be raised either from current or deferred taxes. The full impact of this demand will be felt after 1965, as the pace of new family formation picks up. The amount of public expenditure required to provide streets, sidewalks, street lights, police and fire protection, and all other community facilities to new households far outweighs the amount of public expenditure required to maintain new pupils in elementary school or high school. It is this latter, much greater expenditure which the baby boom will be generating henceforth.

Summary

From whatever perspective we care to view the next twenty-five years, it is clear that the baby boom children, now becoming adults, will create an impact of major proportions. It must be re-emphasized that this impact is predicated upon people already born, and is completely independent of the prospects for longer-run growth. These are the dimly foreseen consequences of fertility upsurge. In our renewed enthusiasm for childbearing and having children, we may have unwittingly created a situation which will cause those children to live at a substantially lower level of comfort and security than was enjoyed by the people who bore them.

It is quite possible that the unmistakable, but as yet small-scale, reduction in fertility that has set in since 1962 may be a mass reaction to the rather unrestrained fertility of the period 1946-60.

The questions we have itemized as public population problems are now being faced in millions of individual households throughout the land, in the form of voting on bonds for high school construction; seeing the rising college tuition rates; having two or three children simultaneously searching for work; needing a larger house that one cannot afford; paying state as well as federal income taxes to build public facilities. Unfortunately for all concerned, the full force of the blow lags about fifteen to eighteen years behind the blessed events that caused it.

POPULATION DISTRIBUTION

Concurrently with its growth the American population has been undergoing a dramatic geographic redistribution. The following shifts are among the most outstanding:

(a) Migration from rural (especially rural-farm) areas has been taking place rapidly.
(b) There has been heavy movement of population toward metropolitan areas.
(c) There has been extensive outward movement from low-income areas to higher income areas of greater economic opportunity.
(d) There has been a flow of middle- and upper-income population from the North and East to the South (especially Florida and the Gulf Coast) and the Southwest.
(e) There has been heavy migration to the Pacific Coast of persons from all strata and from all regions.
(f) There has been massive out-movement of population from the densely settled core of metropolitan areas to the suburban fringe. This movement has become so extensive that the metropolitan areas are beginning to merge one with another, to form extensive chains of megalopolitan proportions, or "conurbations" as the British call them.
(g) There has been a concentration of the Negro population into ghetto-like deteriorated portions of our largest metropolises.

None of these trends is new; all began several decades ago. However, each one has now proceeded to a point where at least some observers are

Map 1

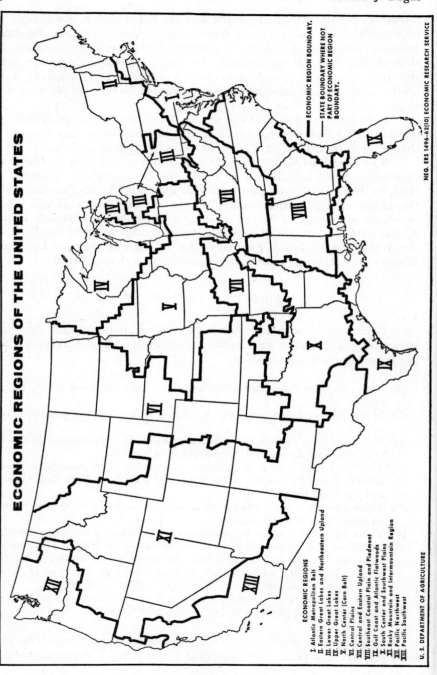

ECONOMIC REGIONS OF THE UNITED STATES

ECONOMIC REGION BOUNDARY.

STATE BOUNDARY WHERE NOT PART OF ECONOMIC REGION BOUNDARY.

NEG. ERS 1496-62(10) ECONOMIC RESEARCH SERVICE

ECONOMIC REGIONS

I Atlantic Metropolitan Belt
II Eastern Great Lakes and Northeastern Upland
III Lower Great Lakes
IV Upper Great Lakes
V North Center (Corn Belt)
VI Central Plains
VII Central and Eastern Upland
VIII Southeast Coastal Plain and Piedmont
IX Gulf Coast and Atlantic Flatwoods
X South Center and Southwest Plains
XI Rocky Mountain and Intermountain Region
XII Pacific Northwest
XIII Pacific Southwest

U. S. DEPARTMENT OF AGRICULTURE

beginning to inquire whether the process has not gone too far or is going too fast. The writer holds no firm opinion about the pattern by which population ought to be distributed for maximal well-being of the nation. It is important, however, to be familiar with the facts and issues, because during the next few decades there will undoubtedly be much discussion of each of these distributional trends.

In presenting the statistical facts about each of these trends, it is necessary to compare one region of the nation with another. A comparatively recent system of regional classification, the system of Economic Regions, has been employed by the Census Bureau and others for more precisely portraying differences in growth patterns from one section of the country to another. The boundaries of these regions are shown in Map 1. Table 3 reports the population and growth rates for each of the thirteen economic regions.

Depopulation of Rural Areas—Between 1950 and 1960 the urban population of the nation increased by twenty-nine per cent, while the rural population declined slightly (one per cent). During this decade, when the nation as a whole was undergoing the greatest population growth in its history, almost one-half (forty-nine per cent) of the 3,134 counties actually *lost* population. These are rural counties and especially counties with large farm populations. Thus, the rural (and especially rural-farm) areas of the nation are in the grip of a great depopulation. This same phenomenon took place in the 1940's, so that in the past two decades many parts of the nation have lost one-fourth to one-half of their 1940 population. The movement has been to cities. At the time of the 1960 census more than seventy per cent of the population was urban and only thirty per cent rural. This phenomenally rapid growth of the urban population has three sources. First, there has been a very great out-migration of people from rural to urban areas, as described above. Second, the urban people have had moderately high birth rates, and have contributed a great deal to their own growth. Finally, small towns grow to a size where they are defined by the census as urban, and subdivisions on the edges of cities are gradually built up solidly enough to be included as a part of the urban population. Between 1950 and 1960 the equivalent of the total migration loss to the rural population, from all sources, seems to have been drawn from the farm population. In 1960 the farm population numbered only 13.4 million, or 7.5 per cent of the total. The exact amount of the loss of farm population between 1950 and 1960 cannot be determined because of a change in the definition of the farm population, but it probably was about six million, or roughly one-fourth of the farm population as of 1950.

How many farmers should we have? Some economists say we still have too many, that the nation's food could be grown on far fewer, more factory-like farms managed by experts using the most scientific methods. Others say we have too few farmers, that the family-size farm is a social

TABLE 3

Distribution of Population by Economic Provinces and Economic Regions, 1950 and 1960; with Measures of Distributional Change, 1950 to 1960.

Province and region	Population 1960 (millions)	Region number	Per cent of total population		Percentage point change	Per cent of population increase 1950-1960	Per cent urban 1960	Per cent rural 1960
			1960	1950				
Total..................	179.0		100.0	100.0	0.0	18.5	69.9	30.1
A. Atlantic Metropolitan Belt Province........	36.5	...	20.3	20.5	−0.2	17.5	86.6	13.4
Atlantic Metropolitan Belt Region...........	36.5	I	20.5	20.5	−0.2	17.5	86.6	13.4
B. The Great Lakes and Northeastern Province.	41.1	...	22.9	23.5	−0.6	15.7	72.5	27.5
Eastern Great Lakes and Northeastern Upland Region..................	10.1	II	5.6	6.1	−0.5	9.7	60.2	39.8
Lower Great Lakes Region...............	25.2	III	14.1	14.1	+0.1	18.6	80.7	19.3
Upper Great Lakes Region..............	5.8	IV	3.2	3.3	−0.1	14.5	58.3	41.7
C. The Midwestern Province..............	23.2	...	13.0	13.5	−0.5	13.6	58.5	41.5
North Center (Corn Belt) Region.........	17.2	V	9.6	10.1	−0.5	12.6	57.9	42.1
Central Plains Region.............	6.0	VI	3.4	3.4	0.0	16.4	60.0	40.0
D. The Southern Province..............	52.1	...	29.0	30.0	−1.0	14.7	56.9	43.1
Central and Eastern Upland Region........	14.9	VII	8.3	9.4	−1.1	5.1	49.9	50.1
Southeast Coastal Plains Region.........	16.4	VIII	9.1	9.9	−0.8	9.6	47.5	52.5
Atlantic Flatwoods and Gulf Coast Region...	11.8	IX	6.6	5.3	+1.3	48.1	76.0	24.0
South Center and Southwest Plains Region..	9.0	X	5.0	5.5	−0.5	8.3	60.4	39.6
E. The Western Province..............	26.5	...	14.8	12.5	+2.3	39.6	78.2	21.8
Rocky Mountain and Intermountain Region.	4.6	XI	2.6	2.4	+0.2	26.7	59.7	40.3
Pacific Northwest Region.............	4.9	XII	2.7	2.7	0.0	21.7	64.4	35.6
Pacific Southwest Region..............	17.0	XIII	9.5	7.5	+2.0	50.1	87.1	12.9

Source: Donald J. Bogue and Calvin L. Beale, *Economic Areas of the United States* (New York: The Free Press of Glencoe, Inc., 1961), Table A, Part I.

institution that we must not abandon. The farm community is reputed to produce wholesome and earnest citizens who suffer less than urban-reared persons from the various personality diseases and, as adults, are more resistant to the disorganizing influences of the big city. Those who hold this philosophy feel that we should preserve the family-farm as a wholesome childrearing as well as a nation-feeding institution. The wholesale consolidation of family-size farms into fewer but larger, more economically "efficient" units has another important side-effect. As the number of farmers decreases, it causes the small town trade centers that served farmers' needs to shrivel up and disappear, so that the whole fabric of rural and small-town social organization is disappearing throughout the rural Midwest, West, and South. Farmers' children must now be hauled dozens of miles on buses to schools, and the farm community is now so dispersed as to be almost nonexistent in many parts of the land. Is it good to have population density in the rural areas decline to a point where community life disappears—especially when the empty rural areas are contrasted with over-full metropolises in which two-hour-long commuting journeys are a part of the daily routine? Do we want somehow to distribute the economy over the land so that we can use our environment for more enjoyable living and reap the personal benefits of freedom and space to be found in a less confined semi-urban location? Has the time come to try to control the urbanward trend in order to preserve some of the culture, character traits, and physical vitality of rural dwellers? These are questions that are being asked by more and more people.

As we become more prosperous as a nation, can we now afford to give greater priority to desirable residential factors in locating the population and less prioriy to the factors of plant-location and a central concentration of business executives? A perfectly uniform distribution of the population over the land is obviously an impractical and probably undesirable goal. The question of how concentrated the population should be is not simple, yet it obviously poses problems for future discussion.

The Metropolitan Shift—For several decades there has been a steady shifting of population to form large urban aggregates that have come to be called "metropolitan areas." The federal government in 1960 recognized 212 of these super-agglomerations as "standard metropolitan statistical areas." Together, these places comprise only a small fraction of the total land area, yet between 1950 and 1960 they hogged eighty-four per cent of the total population increase in the nation. The vast non-metropolitan territory grew only very slowly. This metropolitanization took place in all regions. Thus, the traditionally rural South is now not only urbanized, but is also metropolitanizing rapidly as several of its leading cities accumulate large populations.

This tight agglomeration of the nation's people into a comparatively few very large centers also raises the question of the best location for dwellings in terms of welfare and desirable community life. The present

pattern is forcing a larger and larger share of the work force to travel
long distances to work each day. Billions of dollars are being spent on
expressways and freeways to get people to work in the morning and home
at night. Almost as quickly as such expensive systems are built, they seem
to become clogged with an over-capacity load. It is ironic that only a few
miles outside many of these arteriosclerotic metropolises there are
many small and medium-size cities languishing for want of new industrial
and commercial life. On the one hand, the farm population that once
formed a part of their economic base has been decimated by the new en-
closure movement in agriculture. On the other hand, the recent wave of
corporate mergers and consolidations has killed off many small plants
that were started as local community enterprises but which became
obsolete in the new era of automated industry. City planners are won-
dering whether, in the light of our prospective continued growth, we
should not strive to create a national system of many more small metropolises, more systematically spaced to maximize community living and
minimize congestion, air pollution, problems of water and sewage, and
social problems of crime, delinquency, and social disorganization.

Exodus from Depressed Areas—The delineation of the nation into
economic regions (Map 1) recognized a "Central and Eastern Upland
Region," comprised of the mountainous portions of the southern states.
This region is one of widespread economic hardship and chronic un- and
underemployment. It has comparatively few metropolitan centers, and
many of its industries are depressed. Under the combined impact of the
pull of large metropolitan centers in all directions outside, this area has
suffered a very severe out-migration. Despite the fact that its birth rates
are very high, between 1950 and 1960 it grew at the rate of only 5.1 per
cent, the slowest growth rate for any of the economic regions.

From one point of view, this outmovement may be regarded as a
national gain, since it removes population from a point where it is
unable to earn a livelihood to points where the chances are much improved. But again a question may be raised: might not the long-run interests of less concentrated distribution be better served by undertaking
to develop the region by new industry, better transportation systems, and
improved income distribution than by encouraging the draining off of
population, leaving only limited human resources behind?

In previous decades, another economic region, the Central Plains
Region (Region VI), was denuded of population because of out-migration
in the face of prolonged drought, mechanization of wheat farming, and
farm consolidation. Much of Region IV, the Upper Great Lakes Region,
is a wasteland abandoned after the forests and minerals were exploited.
The same is true of Region II, the Eastern Great Lakes and Northeastern
Upland Region. The rural areas of Region VIII, the Southeast Coastal
Plains and Piedmont Region, are also in a state of chronic depression because of erosion and soil depletion, and the competition of new cotton

lands opened up in the West. All of these regions have been suffering severe population losses to the more prosperous regions.

The solution to the problems of the economically depressed Regions II, IV, VI, VII, and VIII is a topic for major national concern. Together they comprise almost one half of the total land area of the nation. Is it wise to permit or encourage the more prosperous regions to drain them of their population, or should we try to hold the population there and raise its prosperity by some sort of "economic development" of the type we are promoting in Asia, Latin America, and Africa? If we can jar metropolitan Naples, Düsseldorf, and Tokyo out of a state of chronic depression into greater prosperity through selective encouragement of industry, can we do the same for Cairo, Illinois; Charleston, West Virginia; Bangor, Maine; Scranton, Pennsylvania; Pueblo, Colorado; and others?

The In-Movement to the Gulf Coast—One region of the South, the Gulf Coast and Atlantic Flatwoods (Region IX), grew at the phenomenally rapid rate of nearly fifty per cent between 1950 and 1960. It was equalled only by the growth of the Pacific Coast. This sudden build-up along the Gulf Coast has many different components. A part of it is recreation and retirement migration of people seeking to escape the rigors of the northern cold (and with modern air conditioning, to cool them in summer). A part of it is industrial and is based upon growing economic ties with Latin America. A part of it is due to military installations. Most of this flow toward the South is one of middle-income and upper-income groups. The impact upon the economic, political, and social life of the states involved is profound, and this impact has not yet exerted its full force. It has already subverted the old-South political system of Texas and Florida, and may be expected to have similar effects upon Louisiana, Mississippi, Alabama, Georgia and South Carolina. As the coastal development matures, its effect will spread further inland to encompass the lower one-half of each of the states bordering on the Gulf or Atlantic Coast.

This population development is reported not as a "problem" about which we should worry but as a very healthful growth which will help to solve a variety of old population problems. This boom in the Gulf South offers a very important lever for wiping out the last vestiges of the archaic, slavery-based social system. Most of the new Gulf industry is of an inter-state variety. Most of the new employment is of a type which elsewhere is highly unionized. In almost every segment the federal government is the big spender providing much of the impetus. The newly arriving migrants from the North have a lower level of race prejudice. All of these things conjoined could lead, under a long-range policy of nondiscrimination in employment, to an elimination of the caste status for Negroes in the South. Already this development has weakened that system greatly. Just as our economic aid to the nations of Asia, Latin

America, and Africa is promoting the development of a democratic society in those nations, our economic development of the South, and especially the Gulf Coast, can be used to accomplish the same objectives there.

The In-Movement to the Pacific Coast—Region XIII, the Pacific Southwest Region, grew by fifty per cent in the short space of ten years, 1950 to 1960. The entire region from San Francisco and Sacramento in California down the coast and around the southern one-third of Arizona has mushroomed in a most spectacular fashion. The growth is no longer based upon taking advantage of the region's raw resources—gold, agricultural land, and forests. The growth is now entirely urban and metropolitan. Los Angeles is now the nation's second largest metropolis. The State of California has already taken the place of New York as the most populous state of the Union. This dramatic growth has brought problems. The problems of smog and water supply are well known. Less well known and less well appreciated are the problems of economic base. Has this growth been so rapid that it is built upon an economic base that is highly vulnerable to business fluctuations? In the event of a major economic recession would the interior of the nation be flooded with drifting "Cali's" looking for a subsistence in the same way that California was once invaded by "Okies" from the Dust Bowl? The problem is difficult to answer, but it is quite possible that the industrial base of the Pacific Southwest is more vulnerable to the vagaries of the business cycle, the Congressional budget, and technological change than that of any other region in the nation.

The Dying Central City—Almost all of the phenomenal growth that metropolitan areas have been enjoying has been concentrated around their suburban edges. The central cities themselves have grown only very slowly, and almost all of what net growth they achieved between 1950 and 1960 was through annexation. Since the fertility rates in central cities have been moderately high, the failure to grow can indicate only what is well known: the middle class and more well-to-do population have been fleeing to the suburbs in search of more space, more privacy, modern housing, pure air, less delinquency and crime, and neighbors of their own choosing.

This move has created a tremendous building boom in the suburbs. But it has had a most depressing effect upon the central cities themselves. For at least three decades the central cities have been receiving a disproportionately small share of the investments in plants and equipment, new retail ventures, and the construction of residences. As the demand for housing of good quality has eased off, residential properties have been allowed to sink into slum use, with subdivision of living quarters into smaller units, less building maintenance, and less neighborhood upkeep.

Many real estate economists and housing officials actively engaged in "urban renewal" fail to see the direct connection between slum formation and population decline. They tend to blame the influx of low-income incoming migrants. But the fact is that the volume of in-migration is far smaller than the volume of suburbanward out-migration. The phenomenon of community deterioration is everywhere evident, as fine old residential communities which formerly had a high level of community spirit and community integration now degenerate into unorganized masses of obsolescent and under-maintained housing.

The Urbanization of Negroes—For more than a century the rural South has struggled with the problem of Negro-white accommodation following a long era of slave-master arrangements. Suddenly, within the short space of only two decades, the problem has been handed over to urban areas (and particularly the big metropolitan centers) to solve. As recently as 1940 less than one-half of the Negro population was living in cities; a large share was living on farms as sharecroppers or tenants. By 1960, almost three-quarters of the Negro population was urban, and a huge migratory flood of refugees from the collapse of the sharecropper system is continuing to pour into cities—both in the South and the North. Much of this migration has turned westward, so that California and the entire Mountain Region also have large and growing urban Negro populations.

For a very high percentage of Negroes, the movement out of the rural South is advantageous. A substantial share realize a big rise in real income, acquire better housing, have better health and medical care, and can send their children to better schools.

But this population shift has its problematic aspects too. Residential segregation, job discrimination, and differential treatment by community institutions are widely prevalent in the North. Huge Negro ghettos are springing up in our metropolises, and some are beginning to despair that the urban North will be no more successful than the rural South in solving the problem of racial equality. Businesses have capitalized on this race tension, so that Negroes are forced to pay a 10 to 25 per cent "color tax" for housing and many other commodities and services. Often they pay the conventional or established price for goods or services of inferior quality. This seems to be especially true of medical, dental, legal, and other professional services. This is not unlike the exploitation of the sharecropper system.

Yet this shifting of the Negro population from a rural to an urban setting may eventually prove to be the critical event that leads to a resolution of race tension. At the present moment, it is greatly complicating the problem of urban renewal and slum clearance. Under present conditions, the massive arrival of the rural Negroes from the South, bringing with them very high birth rates and a low level of skills for the metropolitan labor market, makes more difficult and more massive the task of rehabilitating the central portions of our cities.

Summary

Quite independently of the problem of total population size, these problems of population distribution pose some very fundamental questions for policy. It should be pointed out that all of these population movements seem to be intimately connected to industrial development, for counterparts of them are found throughout Europe, and are also topics of concern there. The problem has been described in many ways. Perhaps the most general and abstract formulation would be that in all of these economies, prime importance is given to the location and distribution of productive enterprises, and citizens are expected to adjust their residences as best they can to conform to the pattern dictated by the location of jobs.

Recent research has shown that there is very great flexibility in the location of manufacturing and other basic activities. Instead of location being a highly critical consideration, there is a wide range which provides a viable site. Intensive research into the full implications of this fundamental proposition, coupled with imaginative planning, may lead to a national program of population distribution and redistribution which may give us all of the benefits of our modern technology and yet permit us to live in more pleasant environments and in neighborhoods that afford more rewarding living off-the-job.

CONCLUSION

When the demographic facts for the United States are assembled, they suggest that instead of smugly patting ourselves on the back for escaping the impact of the population explosion, we must realize that we are participants. At present we are on a collision course that could lead us to catastrophe, timed to arrive only a very few decades after our sister nations (if they too do not alter their growth rates) have crashed on the Malthusian reefs. There is growing agreement among demographers of the world that rapid population growth does have its costs—wherever it occurs. In the United States it makes it more difficult to make progress, and may lead to a decline in well-being for a substantial share of the population. The fertility holiday in which the United States has indulged herself in the past fifteen years will profoundly affect all aspects of our national life in the next quarter century.

If this unwanted and excessive growth is to be avoided, the fertility limitations needed to stop it must be accepted by the children of today (who are ten years of age and under) when they grow to adulthood and by all future generations of children. Fertility levels are greatly influenced by the family values inherited by children from parents and religious leaders. The time to begin the program of education and guidance which these children need in order to live in the demographic world of the twenty-first century is not the year 2000, but *now*. The drastic change in thinking needed to prepare for this situation on the part of both political and religious leaders should already have been made. The fact that we are only now beginning the process may be a serious matter.

If one accepts these premises, then it is difficult to escape the conclusion that voluntary family limitation with each couple utilizing means that it finds acceptable on religious, aesthetic and physical grounds, is the alternative to some much more radical choices only a few years from now.

In discussions of actions to be taken, one point should be kept clearly in mind: a full solution of the nation's problems of population size can be achieved without requiring dramatic acts of self-restraint or self-denial of the population. A state of zero population growth can be achieved if every person marries and each couple has approximately two children, to replace themselves when they die.

Joseph L. Fisher and Neal Potter

6

Resources in the United States and the World

INTRODUCTION

The question whether resources are becoming scarcer or not has always been significant; it will not be less so in the future. For years, perhaps throughout history, people have been concerned about the relationship between themselves and the land and other resources available to them. As geographic boundaries of regions and continents became known, and as statistical trends of population and agricultural production became established, this concern found more sophisticated and comprehensive expression. Malthus propounded one far-reaching proposition: population tends to outrun the means of subsistence, making preventive checks to population increase desirable and ultimately positive checks necessary. However, the working out of the consequences of the industrial revolution so increased the output of goods and services that Malthus' gloomy prediction has never come true, at least in the Western world.

In more recent times the population explosion in the underdeveloped countries and very rapid increases in most of the more developed places have led to a reawakening of concern about the capacity of the natural environment and its resources to sustain desired rates of economic growth. Science, technology, and the economic adaptation of their accom-

JOSEPH L. FISHER *is President of Resources For The Future, Inc. He has served on several university faculties of economics and as economist and administrative officer of the Council of Economic Advisers. He has published widely on the economics of natural resource development and regional economic analysis.*

NEAL POTTER *is a staff member of Resources For The Future, Inc. He previously served on the faculties of Carnegie Institute of Technology and State College of Washington.*

plishments seem to be pitted dramatically against the sheer increase of population, now running at three per cent a year, or a doubling every twenty-four years, in many less developed areas.

Clearly, the population problem is not simply one of numbers of people, but also of natural resources and how they are used. Much light can be thrown on this by trying to project resource trends into the future and bringing these into juxtaposition with population trends. Of key importance in determining the outcome of the population-resources (or man-land) situation is the kind of technology and culture that is available, including organizational and institutional elements. Population projections, from Malthus to those of the recent past, have been notorious for being far wide of the mark. Projections of natural resources, if anything, have been worse, largely because of the difficulties of projecting technology and institutional adjustments. Nevertheless, some understanding may come from a look at comparative trends in the past, present levels of resource use, and a few projections into the future of a strictly hypothetical nature, however hazardous and uncertain the latter have to be.

Particular attention will be given to certain indicators as to whether natural resources and resource products are becoming scarcer in the United States and other major countries of the world. These indicators are: (1) production and/or consumption of major resource products, especially food and energy; (2) labor productivity trends in resource industries; (3) relative price and/or cost trends for resource commodities compared to trends of prices and/or costs in general; (4) trends in exports and imports, or net foreign trade; (5) trends in the rate of production and use of resources compared to estimated stocks, reserves, or potentials.

These tests of scarcity are applied here to the case of the United States. In the next section they are applied to other continental areas and selected countries. Following this, demand for a number of resource commodities will be projected to the year 2000 for the world and for certain regions and countries. The resource demands will be related primarily to population and productivity trends and will be carried forward on the basis of several hypothetical patterns of improvement in levels of living in various parts of the world. Next there will be a survey of resource reserves and supply alternatives, since new discoveries of sources of supply, technological advances in substitutes, and reduction of waste bear importantly on the question of scarcity. Finally, we shall draw some conclusions from this kind of advance reading of trends toward or away from resource scarcity.

The Case of the United States

It is self-evident that natural resources and their immediately derived products and services are essential to economic growth and well-being.

These things must be sufficiently available either from within a country or by way of imports. In a more highly developed country such as the United States this resource dependency may not always be obvious. The overlay of processed items and varigated economic services often obscures their close connection with resources. But the ultimate dependence on natural resources remains—never far below the surface. Many particular resources are a wasting asset, especially higher quality resources, although the discovery of new sources and the development of substitutes may continue to save us from the consequences of this.

Despite the possibility of altogether new developments, the history of what has happened in the past remains our most reliable guide to the future. Statistics tracing the trends of production, consumption, prices, productivity, and net foreign trade have recently been assembled for resource commodities of the United States.[1] Data are reasonably consistent and reliable from 1870 to the present and can be used in applying the first four tests of scarcity.

Per Capita Consumption

Our first indicator of resource scarcity or abundance is provided by the historical trend of consumption or production of resource commodities on a per capita basis. Chart 1 shows the trends in consumption from 1870 to 1957 for the major resource categories. The over-all trend appears to be steadily upward; only for forest products has the trend been downward.

The aggregates cover up much significant detail. Within the minerals category, for example, oil, natural gas, bauxite, and other items have risen steeply, while since World War I, anthracite and bituminous coal have declined. Among the agricultural products, per capita consumption of wheat and hogs has fallen over the eighty-seven year period, while beef, milk products, and notably citrus fruits have risen. Lumber has declined; pulp and paper have increased.

Labor productivity

The second indicator is the real cost of resource scarcity in terms of labor productivity. Has the cost in human effort of making resource products and services available to the American economy been increasing or not? The employment/output ratio for the resource or extractive industries taken as a whole has been falling consistently for many decades with only an occasional and short-lived interruption. Since the mid-1930's the trend downward has been even more noticeable. This has been true of each of the major resource categories with the notable exception of

---

[1] Taken largely from Neal Potter and Francis T. Christy, Jr., *Trends in Natural Resource Commodities,* Johns Hopkins, Baltimore, 1962.

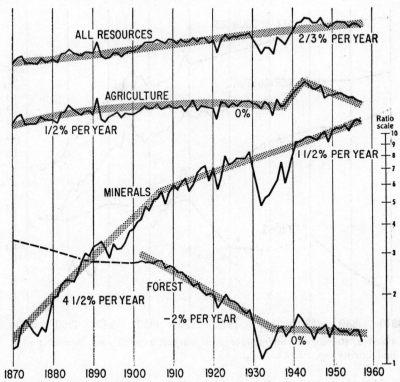

ALL RESOURCES 2/3% PER YEAR

AGRICULTURE 0%

1/2% PER YEAR

Ratio scale

MINERALS 1 1/2% PER YEAR

FOREST

4 1/2% PER YEAR

-2% PER YEAR 0%

Chart 1. Resource sectors: per capita consumption, 1870 to 1957. Source: Potter and Christy, *op. cit.*, Chart 23.

forest products and possibly fish. The employment/output ratio has dropped greatly in agriculture, especially during the past twenty-five years or so. Increases in productivity in agriculture have outstripped those in manufacturing during this period. Chart 2 summarizes these trends.

The number of workers engaged in all the resource industries was seven million—just about the same in 1957 as in 1870. But the value of their output in constant dollars had increased some five times. During the same long period the value of the total national product rose nearly twenty times, with more complex fabrication of raw materials and a larger services component in the expanded economy. In short, about ten per cent of the nation's labor force, instead of over fifty per cent as in 1870, was producing five times as much in resource products and was making possible a gross national product larger still.

According to this very fundamental test—how much work it takes

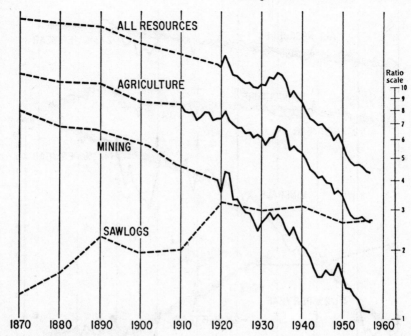

Chart 2. Resource sectors: employment/output, 1870 to 1957. Source: Potter and Christy, *op. cit.*, Chart 45.

to produce resource products and services—resources are not becoming scarcer; quite the opposite, more and more is being produced with less and less labor.

Relative costs and prices

The third indicator is the relative cost or price test. If a resource is becoming scarcer, one would expect the cost of developing or producing derived resource products, and more loosely their prices, to rise compared with prices generally. Statistics in the early period are not thoroughly reliable, but the general picture which emerges, as shown in Chart 3, is that for extractive industries as a whole, prices have moved mostly sidewise since 1870, erratically with many ups and downs and possibly some slight general tendency upward. The component to move upward most noticeably has been forest products, for which relative prices recently have been nearly four times what they were in 1870 and twice those in 1930, although they have not risen particularly since the late 1940's. But the over-all picture does not indicate that resource materials have become scarcer on any general or alarming scale over a good many decades in the past. Technological and economic factors underlying increases in effi-

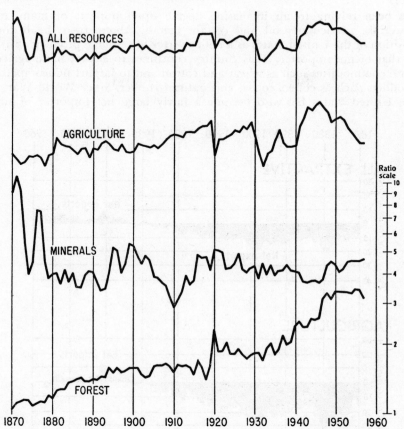

Chart 3. Resource sectors: deflated prices, 1870 to 1957. Source: Potter and Christy, *op. cit.,* Chart 1.

ciency have largely offset tendencies toward greater difficulties and higher costs of extraction. A detailed examination of the long term price trend of copper, for example, after eliminating war years and years in which prices were seriously distorted by cartel arrangements, furnishes evidence that this resource has not followed a course of increasing scarcity, despite a widely help opinion to the contrary. The past is no guarantee of the future, but relative cost and price trends for resources over many past decades do not portend disaster for the next few.

Net imports

The fourth indicator is the resources position of a single country relative to the rest of the world. In more recent years the United States has been relying to an increasing degree upon imports of many raw materials, particularly oil and certain metals. About 1930 the historic position of the United States as a net exporter of resource products shifted to that of net importer. This country continues to export basic agricultural commodities such as wheat and cotton and to import noncompeting products such as coffee, cocoa, and natural rubber. Since World War II, the United States has also become a fairly large net importer of such

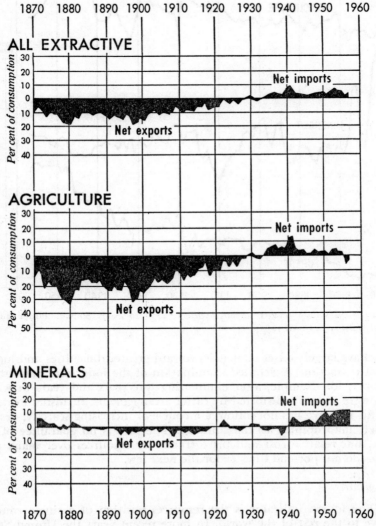

Chart 4. Trends in U. S. foreign trade in resource commodities, 1870 to 1957.

basic items as crude oil and iron ore, while imports of copper, lead, zinc, and certain other metals, already considerable, have continued upward. For the 1956-61 period 17.0 per cent of domestic consumption of crude oil was imported and 25.9 per cent of iron ore.

Chart 4 shows the long term trends of net trade as a per cent of consumption for all extractive industries and for agricultural and mineral products. Without increased imports of particular commodities, costs and prices of certain items in the United States would probably have risen (or have risen more than they did), especially since the Second World War. In some cases new sources or techniques undoubtedly set ceilings to both price rises and amount of imports; for example, oil can be produced from ample reserves of oil shale in the Colorado plateau at only a little above existing oil prices, and low grade taconite ores of which there are large reserves in the Lake States can be utilized. Nevertheless, the fact remains that ready access to foreign supplies has gained in importance to this country. From the viewpoint of national self-sufficiency, certain basic resources have become scarcer, and a larger share of domestic consumption has been imported.

Of these four indicators only one, the import-export test, indicates that resources are becoming scarcer. As far as resource commodities are concerned, the United States has moved to a net import position. This position seems to have remained stable for the past two decades in that net imports as a per cent of total consumption have not continued upward. For minerals, net imports have increased dramatically since World War II, but this has been largely offset by a less dramatic opposite movement in agricultural products, which carry a larger weight in the total picture. Viewed on a world scale in which this country imports raw materials from abroad when they are cheaper, even this test does not indicate increasing scarcity. The other three tests indicate either lessening scarcity, or at least no increase in scarcity, for most items. There are some exceptions, notably lumber (or sawlogs) among the more basic materials. Trends in per capita consumption of resource products, labor productivity trends, and deflated price and cost movements for raw materials—each of these seems to point to the unlikelihood of any general running out of resources in this country for some time to come.[2]

Reserves and potentials for meeting requirements

The fifth indicator, necessarily more speculative than the others, is the comparison of production rates and resource usage with estimates of stocks, reserves, or potentials. A recently completed appraisal for the United States attempts to review the historical data and to look into foreseeable new sources of supply, new technology, populations trends,

[2] Historical data on resource trends have been analyzed carefully in terms of resources-economic growth models in Harold J. Barnett and Chandler Morse, *Scarcity and Growth*, Johns Hopkins, Baltimore, 1963.

and expectations about a rising level of living.[3] On the basis of an estimated increase in population from 180 million in 1960 to 330 in 2000, and an increase in gross national product in 1960 dollars from $503 billion in 1960 to $2,200 billion in 2000, Table 1 shows the increases in a few basic resource and raw material requirements.

In the book from which these estimates are taken, a range of requirements is presented from high to low. The foregoing are medium figures and should be regarded as projections on the basis of assumptions of population, production, income, and the like, all of which are as realistic as a systematic approach would allow.

Regarding capacity to meet these demands, several summary comments may be made. In general, they can be met primarily through new discoveries, technical advances of many sorts, substitutions of cheaper and more plentiful materials, new investment, improved resource management and use, increased imports of certain items, and other activities. As scarcity appears for any one item, pressures will mount to circumvent the consequences; ultimately, if no other solution is found, the cost and price of the item will rise and force an accommodation.

TABLE I

Selected Natural Resources Requirements, 1960 and Projected 2000

	1960	2000
Cropland including pasture (million acres)	447	476
Wheat (million bushels)	1,110	1,385
Cotton (billion pounds)	7	16
Timber (billion cu. ft.)	11	32
Fresh water withdrawal depletions (billion gal. per day)	84	149
East	13.7	37.4
West	59.7	91.7
Pacific Northwest	11.1	20.2
Oil (billion bbls.)	3.2	10.0
Natural gas (trillion cu. ft.)	13.3	34.9
Coal (million short tons)	436	718
Nuclear power (billion kilowatt-hours)	...	2,400
Iron ore (million short tons)	131	341
Aluminum, primary (million short tons)	2.1	13.3
Copper, primary (million short tons)	1.7	4.5

More specifically, cropland will be adequate assuming that yields per acre increase in line with recent trends and as projected. Meeting the increased demand for lumber will strain the country's capacity to produce

[3] Hans H. Landsberg, Leonard L. Fischman, Joseph L. Fisher, *Resources in America's Future*, Johns Hopkins Press, Baltimore, 1963.

saw timber; and perhaps we shall have to resort to additional imports and further substitutions. Improved management of forests and use of products will also be desirable. Water problems are primarily regional; their solution will require more investment in developing supplies and reducing pollution, and more efficient management and use. Petroleum, now in oversupply here and in the world generally, may be short toward the end of the century. Fortunately, there are good possibilities of augmenting underground liquid sources with oil shale and tar sands. Coal reserves remain plentiful. Very large nuclear sources await further reductions in cost. Many nonfuel minerals, while existing abundantly in the earth's crust, involve high extraction and refinement costs. But many areas of the world from which imports can be obtained have not been very well explored, some not at all, and the possibilities of using lower grade ores are reasonably bright. For the minerals especially, it will be important to this country that import capacity is not reduced and that technological progress is continued.

WORLD RESOURCE TRENDS

Having taken this glimpse at the relatively complete historical picture available for the United States, we shall now look at selected parts of the more limited statistical information available for other countries and areas of the world. We shall try to apply to the world data several of the scarcity tests applied in the preceding section, recognizing both the paucity and poor quality of the data for many other parts of the world. In this and the following section our discussion is confined largely to continents and world areas; the accompanying tables show data for selected major countries within the larger areas.

Consumption or output

Looking first at the critical area of food production, it is encouraging to find a Food and Agriculture Organization study concluding that that there has been for the whole world a fourteen per cent increase in per capita food output since the prewar period.[4] This seems to indicate an improved future for the world's hungry people.

When we examine the picture more closely, however, we find serious problems. Per capita food output in Latin America, Asia, and Africa is no better than it was twenty-five years ago—progress has occurred almost exclusively in North America, Western Europe, and the Soviet Union. During the 1950's the picture was brighter for Latin America and especially for non-Communist Asia. Moreover, the areas which have lagged contain two-thirds of the world's population, and have notoriously poor diets. The lag seems to be partly the result of rapid rates of population growth, and partly the failure of these areas (except perhaps Mexico and Japan) to participate sufficiently in the agricultural revolution that has

[4] *State of Food and Agriculture 1962*, p. 16.

brought such large increases in output per man and per acre in North America and Western Europe.

The rate of increase is only part of the picture and should be complemented by data on levels of consumption. Rough and partial data on per capita consumption of calories shows that Northern America and Western Europe consume about fifty per cent more than the least developed areas. This difference is not as great as one might expect, but it means partial starvation for a majority in the poorest nations. More serious is the protein and vitamin deficiency which is not reflected in calorie data.

Chart 5, borrowed from an FAO study, portrays the diets in different areas in terms of their values, (i.e., the sums of the price-weighted farm commodities used for food in each region). It can be seen that this way of looking at food facts gives the Far East a diet about one sixth as valuable as that in North America (indexes of about 51 and 312, respectively, where 100 equals the world average for the years 1948-52). Western Europe, which on a calorie basis is ninety-four per cent as well off as North America, is by this "value" comparison only about sixty per cent as well off. As can be seen by the shaded portions of the bars in the chart, most of the differences arise in the values of livestock products (meat, milk, eggs, etc.) consumed. Large increases in the proteins supplied by such products are required for an adequate diet in the underdeveloped parts of the world; but of course minimum nutritional standards can be met by a level of consumption well below the average for North America.

To summarize the food output picture, it appears that while the past twenty-five years have shown a moderate improvement, there is still a long way to go, and progress is least where it is needed most.

The second most important of the available indexes of materials supply is that for mineral and hydroelectric energy consumption. Here the rates of growth are more encouraging than those for food. Not only do the trends incline more steeply upward (one and three-quarter per cent per year instead of one-half per cent per year), but growth seems generally steeper in areas where consumption is lowest. Thus Western Europe and the United States show increases of only nineteen and thirty-six per cent for 1937-60, while non-Communist Asia shows thirty-nine per cent, Africa over 100 per cent, and Latin America and the Soviet Union over 150 per cent. It is well to note, however, that the range of disparities in energy consumption among different countries are of the order of 100-to-1, whereas in food values they are only on the order of 6-1 (Chart 5) and in calories less than 2-to-1.

For energy we have a picture that is clearly brightening, with the increase tending to concentrate in the poorer areas; but the distance to the standards of the advanced countries is very great.

Among nonfuel minerals, variations in rate of growth among countries have been wide. The increase in world output of iron ore during

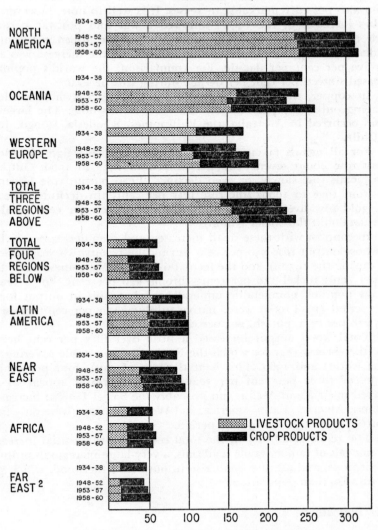

(PRICE-WEIGHTED INDICES, WORLD[1] AVERAGE FOR ALL FOOD, 1948-52 = 100)

[1] EXCLUDING U.S.S.R., EASTERN EUROPE AND MAINLAND CHINA.
[2] EXCLUDING MAINLAND CHINA.

Chart 5. Estimated per capita food supplies, by world regions, prewar to 1958-60. Source: FAO, State of Food and Agriculture, 1961, page 30.

the 1950's was nearly 100 per cent, with rates of increase in some of the less developed areas, such as Latin America and non-Communist Asia, running to several hundred per cent. Western Europe and the Soviet Union also posted remarkable increases. It is well to note, however, that the big increases of the 1950's followed a war and postwar period in which the rate of increase was quite low—about fifteen per cent per decade. For the period 1937-60 taken as a whole, the increase was about forty-five per cent per decade. For comparison, the world's population increased sixteen per cent per decade during this period.

In copper, the rate of growth in the 1950's was more moderate, averaging only sixty per cent for the world as a whole. The largest increases occurred in Australia, the Philippines, Rhodesia, Congo, Japan, and Chile.

For all metals taken together, the world price weighted index of output rose about seventy-two per cent from 1938 to 1960. Output of some metals rose slowly, or even declined. Lead output rose fifteen per cent from 1938 to 1960; zinc rose fifty per cent; tin declined three per cent; gold rose five per cent; silver declined fifteen per cent (gold and silver data omit the Soviet Union).

In contrast with these small increases, and even decreases, are bauxite, whose output rose 550 per cent during the twenty-two years (210 per cent during the 1950's), and the ferroalloy metals. Manganese output rose 120 per cent; nickel 150 per cent; chrome 220 per cent. For a few significant nonfuel, nonmetallic minerals, the increases in output for this same period (1938-1960) were: native sulphur, 130 per cent; phosphate rock, 210 per cent, potash, 205 per cent.

Total wood output increased a little over fifty per cent between 1946 (the earliest year for which the FAO presents a table covering most of the world) and 1960. This is at the rate of thirty-four per cent per decade, or three per cent per year. Largest increases appear to have occurred in Asia and Africa, and probably the Soviet Union; increases in Northern America, Latin America, and Western Europe were only fifteen to thirty per cent in the 1946-60 period.

The relative stability in the total conceals a substantial increase in the removals of lumber-grade materials, a very large increase in pulpwood and pitprops, and a quite small rise in output of fuelwood, which probably rose less than population.

Other indicators

World data for the remaining scarcity indicators are even scantier but permit some analyses and conclusions. By reason of space limitations only the conclusions reached are presented. The second indicator, the employment-output ratio, shows an improving trend in the raw materials industries which should support rising levels of living. The figures on agriculture look quite encouraging. While they reflect the strong upsurge in productivity in North America and Western Europe resulting from the agricultural revolution which occurred in the past twenty-five years, declines in labor required per unit of output also appear to be substantial in Latin America, Asia and Africa. Mining labor required per unit of output for the world as a whole declined twenty-nine per cent on the average between 1938 and 1953. While the improvements in Western Europe and Asia were not great in this period, it seems probable that much greater improvements have occurred since 1953.

Relative prices are our third test of scarcity trends. Here we run into a morass of changing value standards, fluctuating exchange rates, and artificially fixed or supported prices; yet a few series are available which appear to be reasonably good indicators. They relate chiefly to a few standard commodities which have been traded on a fairly free world market over the past fifty years or so. We have analyzed four of these. The constant dollar prices of wheat and sugar have fallen by about one half since the days preceding World War I; cotton has fallen about twenty per cent, and copper by twenty-five to forty per cent.

Some individual country indexes and a world index which average together a wide range of food and raw materials prices have also been analyzed. While the world index of the export prices of raw materials shows a marked rise from 1938 to 1953 and a persistent fall thereafter, it appears that there were many different trends in relative prices in individual countries during this short period.

Series of deflated world prices for the four items indicate lessening relative scarcity over a long period. The more aggregative indexes indicate increasing relative scarcity for the period 1938-1960 (especially 1938-1953), and perhaps decreasing scarcity since 1953. No clear trend seems to be established at this time, and therefore this test is inconclusive as a guide to the future.

Fourth, we examined also the growth of trade in raw materials as an indicator of scarcity, not from the viewpoint of the whole world, of course, but from the viewpoint of particular areas. FAO indexes show a forty-one per cent increase in total world imports of food and foodstuffs since the prewar period, and an increase of over fifty per cent in the past ten years. The biggest changes came in the shift of North America from a small net import balance, due largely to the droughts of the 1930's, to large net exports, and the shift of the Near East and Asia from small net exports to large net imports.

In bread grains, especially wheat and rye, little change in the balance of trade took place between 1934-38 and 1960 for Europe, the Soviet Union, or Oceania. But North America increased its exports very heavily (in 1960 U. S. net exports of these grains were forty-seven per cent of output), while Asia imported half the increased exports, and South America and Africa absorbed small amounts. In feed grains (corn, barley, oats and sorghum) Europe has absorbed a good portion of the increased exports, while Asia, being still very poor, has imported little, for keeping livestock is a relatively expensive business. South America is not yet on a net import basis in feeds, but has reduced its exports over one half.

Oil and oilseeds data show North America shifting from net imports to net exports, Africa making a precisely opposite change, while Asia and South America have reduced their net exports and Europe is absorbing increased imports.

Trade in other raw materials is considerably smaller than that in agricultural products. In 1960 world food and "raw materials" imports totalled $39.5 billion. The next largest group of resource materials was fuels, totalling $10.8 billion. However, while the values are smaller, the rate of increase in international fuel trade is more steeply upward than that for food and raw materials: 1960 fuel trade was 170 per cent above 1938 and 80 per cent above 1950.

It may be well to note not only the sharp rate of growth in fuels trade, but the fact that a number of nations are almost wholly dependent on imports for their energy supplies, while other nations are thoroughly dependent on exports for their national prosperity. In 1960, Italy, for example, produced only thirty-one per cent of its energy needs; Sweden, sixteen per cent; Philippines, seven per cent; Puerto Rico, one per cent. Venezuela's 1960 exports were ninety per cent petroleum and products; Iraq's ninety-seven per cent; for Iran, the figure was seventy-four per cent in 1958.

The net import test, therefore, presents a variety of pictures, country by country, but generally of increasing dependence on sources or markets in other countries. For the world as a whole increasing dependence, or linkage, among the countries for their raw materials should result in lower costs generally speaking, and, therefore, increases in living levels, as fuller advantage is taken of more favorable international locations of resources.

CONCLUSION

It has not been possible to assemble historical data in a comprehensive way to show resource trends in the other world areas as was done for the United States. The foregoing effort to examine such selected evidence as could be brought readily to hand is far from conclusive. But it does warn against easy generalizations that the rest of the world is about to run out of raw materials on the one hand or, on the other, that the less developed areas are going to take off right away into rapid improvements in living levels because of plentiful supplies of food, energy and raw materials. The picture is mixed: quite favorable for energy commodities, less so for food. As with the United States, only more dramatically, much will depend on the rate at which technological advances already proven can be broadly applied, and on keeping open the channels of world trade.

PROJECTIONS OF WORLD RESOURCE DEMANDS

Let us now take a look at levels of demand for resource and raw materials which would arise by the year 2000 under a few simple assumptions. Taking the population projections of the United Nations, Table 2,

TABLE 2

Population Trends: Historical 1920-1960, and Projections 1980 and 2000,
by World Areas (millions)

	1920	1938	1950	1960	1980	2000
					(UN medium projections)	
World........................	1811	2170[5]	2510	2995	4220	6280
North America..................	117	143	167	199	254	312
Latin America..................	91	125[e]	162	206	348	592
Western Europe.................	246[e]	265[e]	286	307	360[e]	400[e]
Eastern Europe & U.S.S.R.......	250[e]	290[e]	279[e]	332	440[e]	550[e]
China, Communist Asia..........	460[e]	500[e]	590[e]	710[e]	1040[e]	1600[e]
Non-communist Asia.............	500[e]	680[e]	790[e]	970	1430[e]	2300[e]
Africa.........................	141	169[e]	206	254	333	517
Oceania........................	8.8	11.0[e]	13.0	16.5	22	29

[5] 1937
[e] —rough estimates by the authors.
Sources: UN, *Demographic Yearbook*, 1956, 1961; UN, *The Future Growth of World Population* (Population Studies, No. 28, 1958); UN, *Statistical Yearbook*, 1957, 1961; and others; plus estimates of the authors, involving minor adjustments or extrapolations of UN data.

we have made rough estimates of the materials which would be consumed in the year 2000 under the following assumptions:

1. The trends of the decade of the 1950's continue for the next four decades in the several parts of the world.
2. The average per capita level of consumption for the world as a whole in the year 2000 is at the level attained in the United States in 1960.[6]
3. The average level of consumption in the world is at the level attained by Western Europe in 1960.

[6] This appears to omit an allowance for rising standards in the United States, but the omission is not large, since U. S. population is projected at only four and one-half per cent of the world total; and increases in per capita consumption of raw materials in the United States recently have been only about one-third per cent a year.

4. The United States, Europe, the Soviet Union, and Oceania consume at the rate of the United States in 1960, while the rest of the world attains the level of Western Europe in 1960.

Food Products

Applying these four assumptions to the available data on food:

1. The world production indexes of the FAO show an increase in per capita food output of fourteen per cent between the 1948-52 average and 1960.[7] In four decades, this rate of increase would compound to nearly seventy per cent.

2. An increase in average per capita calorie consumption of the world to the level attained by the United States in 1960 would involve a thirty-eight per cent increase. The increase in proteins and other food elements would be much larger, but we shall discuss this later.

3. The increase in world per capita consumption of calories to attain a West European 1960 level would be thirty per cent.

4. If North America, Europe, the Soviet Union, and Oceania consumed at the 1960 levels of the United States, and the rest of the world consumed at West European 1960 levels, world per capita caloric intake would be thirty-two per cent above its actual 1960 level.

In Table 3 we summarize the caloric food values which would be produced or consumed under each of the above assumptions as to the changes in per capita output or consumption, when combined with the total population projections of Table 2. Thus the world total per capita output in 2000 would be seventy per cent above the 1960 levels and population 110 per cent over 1960. Combined, these percentages give an increase of 260 per cent. The 6,800 trillion 1960 world total calorie intake, increased by 260 per cent, is the 24,000 trillion calories shown in column (1) for the world.

It is most interesting that the rise in output trends of the 1950's should give us a projection of year 2000 output which is higher than any of the three consumption "goals" set forth in assumptions 2, 3, and 4. This does not mean, however, that an adequate diet is assured for the world's hungry people, because:

> First, there are very great difficulties in maintaining for forty years a rate of increase achieved for ten years, particularly when the ten years included a significant amount of recovery from wartime damage and neglect in Europe, the Soviet Union, and Japan, as well as considerable impact from recent agricultural discoveries, such as DDT, 2-4D, and hybrid corn.

[7] U. N. Food and Agricultural Organization, *State of Food and Agriculture 1962*, p. 14. The FAO has not published data showing the growth of food consumption during this decade, so we have used the output indexes instead.

TABLE 3

Projections of Total Food Calories for the Year 2000 Compared to 1960 Actual for World Areas (Trillions per Day)

	1960 Actual	Total calorie output in 2000 if trend of 1948/52 to 1960 continues (1)	Total calorie consumption in the year 2000 if:		
			World is at U. S. 1960 level of consumption (2)	World is at West Europe 1960 level (3)	N. Am., Eur., USSR, and Oceania at U. S. 1960; rest at Europe 1960 level (4)
World..............	6,800	24,000	19,600	18,500	18,800
North America.......	620	1,310	970	920	970
Latin America.......	520	1,670	1,850	1,750	1,750
Western Europe......	910	3,450	1,250	1,180	1,250
Eastern Europe and USSR............	850°	5,000	1,700	1,600	1,700
Communist Asia.....	1,300°	4,700?	5,000	4,700	4,700
Non-Communist Asia.	1,900°	6,900	7,200	6,800	6,800
Africa..............	600°	1,500	1,600	1,500	1,500
Oceania............	53	140	90	85	90

° —rough estimates by the authors.
? —guess by the authors.
Source: See text, Section IV for derivation of projections.

Second, there are much larger and more serious deficiencies in proteins and vitamins and other values in the world's average diet. While the world needs only a thirty to forty per cent increase in per capita calorie intake, it needs a fifty to seventy-five per cent increase in its protein supply to reach West European standards of 1960. The increase in animal proteins (milk, eggs, meat, etc.) required would be of the order of 500 per cent.

A considerable portion of this 500 per cent increase in animal proteins would be needed to give a nutritionally adequate diet for most of Asia and Africa, and much of Latin America. Moreover, these proteins are costly in terms of the crops and pasture lands required to produce them. The calorie-to-protein conversion ratios require complex calculations which we do not attempt here. However, if we may judge by comparing the over-all costs of diets in Western Europe and the underdeveloped continents, nearly a 100 per cent increase in the value of world food output is needed to supply a nutritionally adequate diet.

If a 100 per cent rise in dietary levels is to be provided for a world population which is 110 per cent larger in the year 2000 than it was in 1960, output would have to rise by 320 per cent. This is more than a quadrupling of output, and is considerably higher than the 260 per cent increase which would be provided if the 1950-60 rate of increase in per capita output could be maintained for the next four decades (Table 3, Col. 1).

In Table 4 we have projected consumption for the year 2000 on the basis of the same four assumptions that were employed in the foregoing discussion of food. Taking the various estimates together, it looks quite

TABLE 4

Projections of Energy Consumed in 2000 Compared to 1960 Actual by World Areas
(Billions of metric tons of coal equivalent)

	1960 Actual	Year 2000 if:			
		Trend in consumption from 1950 to 1960 continues (1)	World consumption is at U. S. 1960 level (2)	World consumption is at W. Europe 1960 level (3)	N. Am., Eur., USSR, & Oceania at U. S. 1960; rest at Europe 1960 level (4)
World..............	4.2	20.8	50.3	16.1	23.2
North America.......	1.55	2.56	2.50	.80	2.50
Latin America.......	.14	2.89	4.74	1.52	1.52
Western Europe......	.79	2.77	3.20	1.03	3.20
Eastern Europe & USSR............	.90	4.5	4.40	1.41	4.40
Communist Asia......	.40	4.5?	12.8	4.1	4.1
Non-Communist Asia.	.24	2.7	18.4	5.9	5.9
Africa..............	.08	.77	4.14	1.33	1.33
Oceania............	.05	.10	.23	.07	.23

? —guess by the authors.
Source: See text, for derivation of projections.

possible that the year 2000 world consumption of energy will be about five times that of 1960, or more roughly, four to six times as great. World consumption of energy in 2000 at the 1960 U. S. level appears unattainable, although rates of increase in other parts of the world, especially the less developed areas, are expected to exceed greatly that of the U. S. during the next forty years.

Continuation for the next four decades of the phenomenal growth in iron ore output which occurred in the 1950's would produce a fourteenfold increase, or nearly a seven-fold increase per capita. This is roughly the same as the U. S. rate of increase during its forty years of fastest growth in production of iron, and thus seems like a possible rate of growth for much of the world, despite its steepness. However, it seems unlikely that these recent rates of growth in output for Latin America, the Soviet Union, and Asia can continue for forty years. Moreover, they would yield a world consumption of one-half ton per capita as compared to U. S. 1960 consumption of one-third ton, and Western Europe's per capita of one-sixth ton. A six-fold increase would provide a world per capita consumption of one-quarter ton, which seems to be a more reasonable projection.

The growth in output projected for copper at the 1950-60 rate is very modest compared to that of the United States during its "take-off" forty year period—about six-fold compared to nearly forty-fold. Nevertheless, the fact that the older producing areas, like the United States, Chile, and Europe, show slower rates of growth, plus the fact that the 1937-60 growth was only sixty-five per cent (twenty-five per cent per decade) indicate difficulties may be in store for even a six-fold increase. Furthermore, aluminum is now available for important uses formerly met solely by copper.

For want of space, we merely mention a number of other significant minerals. Summarizing, it appears that the growth rates of ferroalloys may be about as high as for iron, while a much higher rate of growth in the case of bauxite seems inevitable as the use of aluminum continues to expand rapidly in construction, transportation equipment, and electrical goods. Other metals may experience a slower rate of growth than during the recent past. Such nonmetals as sulfur, phosphate, and potash may experience fairly high rates of growth—several hundred per cent over the forty years as fertilizer and other chemical industries grow.

Forest products

The increase in the rate of wood removals from the forests of the world between 1946 and 1960 was about fifty per cent. Projected for the next forty years, this rate of increase would mean another 200 per cent increase in the rate of cutting. Even the fifty per cent rate of increase for the past period has been moderated by the inclusion of fuelwood in the total. Sawlogs cutting increased sixty-six per cent in the fourteen years 1946-60; projected for forty years this gives an increase of 300 per cent. The pulpwood-pitprop class would increase over 600 per cent at the 1946-60 rate of growth. In view of the level trend in consumption of sawlogs in the United States in the past fifty years, and the sharp rate of increase in prices, we feel no assurance that these world forest product projections will actually be experienced. Will it be possible to increase the output of food, energy, wood products, minerals, and other raw materials so as to reach the levels projected in the preceding section? By the year 2000 this would involve approximately:

1. A quadrupling of aggregate food output, including adequacy of proteins and vitamins.
2. A five-fold increase in energy output.
3. Perhaps as much as a six-fold increase in output of iron ore and ferroalloys, and somewhat less in copper, and a very much larger increase in bauxite-aluminum.
4. A possible quadrupling of lumber output, and a seven-fold increase in pulpwood and pitprops.

Food

The most important of these required increases and the most difficult to meet is probably that in food output.

The chief hope of reaching the food "target" lies in increasing yields per acre. The first three columns of Table 5 show increases in yields for some of the principal crops as estimated by the FAO for the 1950's. The average increase in yields on a world basis for these principal crops— chiefly grains—was something like twenty-five per cent for the decade. Thus, increases in yields per acre seem largely to account for the increase of thirty-five per cent in the total food output for this decade, as estimated by the FAO.[9] A twenty-five per cent per decade increase, if it were maintained for forty years, would raise the output of food about 140 per cent, less than half what is needed to quadruple output.

If, instead of the world average, one looks only at the rate of increase in yields for the parts of the world which underwent great agricultural progress in this decade (Europe and Northern America), one notes rates of increase running at thirty-three per cent and up for the important grains, except rice (Table 5). A thirty-five per cent increase for each of four decades would give an aggregate increase of 230 per cent, which is considerably less than the projected increase of 320 per cent which we concluded previously would be necessary to feed the year 2000 population at an "adequate" standard.

Thus, even on fairly optimistic projections of yield increase, we achieve an output index of 330 (230 + 100) as against a "goal" index of 420. What other sources of increase in food output may there be?

The second major way to increase food production is by increasing the area of land cultivated. The FAO *Production Yearbook*[10] reports something over 300 million hectares as "unused but potentially produc-

[9] *State of Food and Agriculture 1962*, p. 14. It should be noted that mainland China is included in the estimates of yields, while the estimates of total food output exclude China.
[10] 1961, Table 1.

TABLE 5

Changes in Crop Yields Per Acre, by Major Crops for Selected World Areas

	% Increase in Yields	1960 over 1948-52		N. America & Europe ÷ Asia, Latin America, and Africa (1960)
	World	Europe	North & Central Am.	
Wheat..................	22	25	42	1.99
Rye....................	29	20	53	2.15
Barley.................	31	45	11	2.31
Oats...................	16	21	22	1.95
Maize.................	29	80	31	2.83
Millet and sorghum......	43	(1)	94	4.49
Rice..................	24	−4	24	2.49
Potatoes...............	5	13	26	1.82
Sweet potatoes and yams..	−3	(1)	17	.91
Cotton................	33	107	56	2.26

(1) very small quantities produced.

Source: FAO, *Production Yearbook 1961*, Tables 10A and 10B.

tive." This is about twenty per cent of the area listed as "arable and under crops." A twenty per cent increased area, yielding 230 per cent more output per acre, would yield an output index of 400, quite near our target of 420.

It seems probable, in addition, that some of the 4,000 million hectares now listed as "forested" could be cultivated. There are also 2,600 million hectares of "permanent meadows and pastures" and over 5,000 million hectares of "built-on areas, waste land, and other" which may provide some additions to arable land, given new means of cultivation, irrigation, and drainage. In short, with little more than ten per cent of the world's land area under crops, we may hope for substantial increases when need and ingenuity are brought to bear on the more favorable parts of the remaining ninety per cent.

In addition, there is almost a "quantum jump" possible in the output of some of the backward areas of the world, if their lands can be made to yield at the same rate as those of Northern America and Europe. Yields from the latter are generally double those of Asia, Africa, and Latin America. Doubling the yields for sixty per cent of the non-Communist world's grain acreage where yields are now low would increase world output of grain by sixty per cent.

What is required to secure these large increases in yields? The matter is complex and includes some relatively unchangeable factors like climate and soil qualities; but large possibilities seem to center on the use of more adequate amounts of fertilizer, improved cultivation and harvesting practices, proper use of irrigation water, and use of better seeds and pesticides. More efficient tenure, credit, and marketing methods can also play an important part. Some of these factors, such as more fertilizer, require significant amounts of capital investment; others do not. Better extension services and a willingness to change long established farming practices can also make significant contributions. Both capital and technical assistance programs can do a great deal to help in achieving adequate food output for an expanding world population.

Energy

The problem of increasing energy output is complicated by the fact that mineral fuels are wasting assets; that is, there are fixed quantities in existence, and replenishment is at a geological pace, infinitesimally slow relative to the rate of use. Knowledge of reserves is quite scanty, chiefly because there is insufficient incentive to do expensive exploration work until there is prospective use or market within the next one to three decades. All future values in the market place are subject to discount at the going rate of interest (A five per cent rate of discount makes a dollar, 50 years hence worth only nine cents today).

Speculative estimates, based on general knowledge of geological formations around the world, and on rates of occurrence of coal seams, oil and gas fields, and oil shale, give conventional energy reserves equal to about 900 years of use at the 1960 rate of consumption, or 150-200 years of consumption at the rate foreseen for the year 2000.[11]

Others regard this as optimistic, or at least they anticipate that many areas of the world will have to rely mainly on nuclear energy in less than a century if steeply increased costs and reductions in consumption are to be avoided.[12]

Even 150-200 years seem like a shockingly short time for the world to use up its entire stock of fossil fuels. However, we can be sure that rises in costs of obtaining energy commodities as they become scarcer will stimulate exploration and technical research and development and will dampen further increases in demand. Moreover, alternate energy sources, particularly atomic fission and perhaps fusion, will play an important part.

By the year 2000, ten to twenty per cent of the world's energy consumption may be taken care of by atomic plants, principally through providing heat for the generation of electricity.[13] This degree of substitu-

---

[11] *Fossil Fuels in the Future,* by Milton F. Searl (U. S. Atomic Energy Commission, October 1960), pages 1-9.

[12] H. J. Bhabha, Chairman, Indian Atomic Energy Commission, Address Before Second Plenary Session, U. N. Conference on the Application of Science and Technology for the Benefit of Less Developed Areas, Geneva, 1963.

[13] Projections made recently for the United States show that by 2000 about fifteen per cent of total energy may come from nuclear sources, and about half of all electricity generation. From then on, nuclear energy is expected to furnish increasing proportions of both. See Landsberg, Fischman, Fisher, *op. cit.*

tion would enable the world to stretch out its reserves of fossil fuels to last perhaps 200 or 250 years instead of 150 or 200. However, it seems clear that neither the rate of energy use nor the rate of substitution of atomic sources will remain constant at the projected year 2000 rates. The question is, which will increase faster, energy consumption, or the rate of output from atomic sources?

The answer to this question depends on the relative costs of fossil fuels and atomic energy and on possibilities for substitution now foreseen only dimly. Projections for the United States indicate that, on balance, the use of fossil fuels will continue to increase after the year 2000; that atomic fuels are not likely to be sufficiently used to take care of all of the increased consumption of energy. Thus, fossil fuels may become a very serious problem in the United States within a century, and drastic measures of substitution may become necessary.[14]

Are the the resources of atomic fuels sufficient to meet these projected requirements? This question cannot be answered with much assurance at the present time because atomic technology is still in its infancy, and great increases in economically usable reserves are foreseen, as well as large increases in efficiency of using these reserves. One recent writer conjectures that existing "economically recoverable" supplies of uranium in the United States by the year 1980 may be able to produce as much as 4,100 quadrillion Btus. or about fifty per cent as much as the total United States reserves of fossil fuels.[15] This would depend on major advances in atomic technology in the next twenty years, but it does not allow for large possibilities in the use of plutonium as a fuel. And possibly of far greater importance, it takes no account of the possibility that an atomic fusion process may make practical the use of hydrogen as a fuel source, which would vastly increase atomic energy reserves.

Nonfuel minerals

As we have observed previously, discovery and "proving up" of reserves of minerals is rarely done for more than the use expected within two or three decades. However, enough is known in a rough sort of way to provide fair degrees of assurance as far at least as the year 2000.

A recent study indicates that for iron, aluminum, and manganese, at least, the known and inferred reserves are large enough, world-wide, to supply all projected demands for at least the next forty years without a significant increase in costs.[16] This would hold true even if the rapid rates of growth of the 1950's continue. For copper, lead, and zinc, however, the

[14] Searl, *op. cit.,* pp. 6-10.
[15] Philip Mullenbach, *Civilian Nuclear Power* (New York; Twentieth Century Fund, 1963), p. 119.
[16] Bruce C. Netschert and Hans H. Landsberg, *The Future Supply of the Major Metals: A Reconnaissance Survey* (Resources for the Future, 1961).

demands which seem likely are expected to use all known economic reserves by the year 2000. Either large new discoveries of ore bodies, considerable advances in technology, or very large increases in prices will be required to take care of the increased demands which will be experienced if anything like the 1950-1960 rate of growth continues. It should be kept in mind, however, that there are good substitutes for these metals in many uses, and that substitution and technology will proceed at an accelerated pace if cost increases do indeed occur.

Forest products

Whether the world's forests will be able to stand the drains projected above seems dubious, though much information is required to make a conclusive judgment. We do know, however, that in the United States the relative price of lumber has risen by 300 per cent since 1870; and the U. S. Forest Service warns that the projected rate of cutting over the next forty years considerably exceeds growth, particularly for trees of saw timber grade.[17]

On the world scene, one hopeful landmark should be noted. Data on land use indicate that half the world's output of sawlogs and forty per cent of its total wood came from North America and Western Europe in 1960; yet the forested acreage in these two areas is only a little over twenty per cent of the world's total. Thus, if sustained output in the rest of the world can be brought to a European-American level, it would allow for a doubling of output. Large, relatively untapped forests exist in tropical and subarctic regions. Substitute materials are also available; for example, steel, aluminum, and building blocks.

In addition, only moderately costly changes in management could yield a large increase even in United States output, especially in small private ownership areas. In less developed areas, where cutting practices are poorer than in this country, the gains from this source could be much greater.

International trade in lumber, pulp, and paper has been and can continue to be extensive so that the world outlook is important for most countries. Nevertheless, areas with poor indigenous forests and little capacity to import forest products will obviously have difficulty.

Water

In this paper we have not gone into the United States or the world outlook for water demand and supply. Comprehensive historical data for this country are very limited and are virtually non-existent for many parts of the world. Shortage of water that can be made available at reasonable

[17] *Timber in America's Future* (U. S. Government Printing Office, 1958), especially pp. 96 ff.

cost severely limits economic development in many arid and semi-arid areas. Water occurrence unfortunately is irregular in most countries, both regionally and seasonally. Furthermore, water is costly to transport, prohibitively so for long distances.

Estimates of water demand and supply by continents, or even by countries except for the very smallest, make little sense; the job has to be done by river basins and frequently by portions of basins. However, some rough estimates made recently for the United States indicate that withdrawal depletions of water have been rising fairly rapidly and will continue to do so in the future. (Withdrawal depletions consist of fresh water taken from streams and lakes and not returned.) Withdrawal depletions in the East are estimated to increase from 13.7 billion gallons per day in 1960 to 37.4 in 2000; in the more arid West from 59.7 to 91.7; and in the Pacific Northwest from 11.1 to 20.2.[18] Much of the increase will be for industrial uses. Large additional amounts, not actually depleted, but frequently rendered unavailable for other uses, will be required to dilute pollutants and carry them downstream.

A number of possibilities exist for augmenting supplies. Additional storage reservoirs can be constructed; evaporation and irrigation canal losses can be checked; water-consuming trees and plants can be reduced; water can be recycled in industry; salt or brackish water can be substituted for fresh water in cooling and some other uses; water prices can be raised to check increases in consumption; surface and ground water sources can be integrated for more economic use; whole river systems can be inter-connected. Demineralization of brackish and even ocean water can be done by several different methods at costs which are already competitive, or nearly so, in a few remote places. Pollution abatement on many streams would yield large amounts of higher quality and, therefore, more usable water than is now available. Large gains could be made by legal and institutional changes which would result in some reallocation of water use away from irrigation, toward industrial and other much higher value uses. For the United States water requirements for the next four decades should be met without too much difficulty, save for a few places, if a number of these supply-increasing and loss-reducing efforts are applied with reasonable success.

Western Europe, also a highly developed area, for the most part has ample rainfall so that, with additional investment and careful management, future needs should be met. The same appears to be true for Japan, although in both these areas development will have to be more intensive and management careful. More effective institutional arrangements than in the United States have made possible heavy concentrations of population and water-using industries in the Ruhr valley of West Germany, despite limited amounts of fresh water.

[18] Landsberg, Fischman, Fisher, *op. cit.*

For the less developed areas we have not gathered data to support general conclusions of the type presented here. Obviously water is short in some places and at some periods of the year, while it is too plentiful in other places and times. In many of the more arid areas, such as West Pakistan, North Africa, and Northeast Brazil, agricultural improvement will depend heavily on water developments of various kinds. Cheap demineralization obviously would be a boon in such places as these; to date costs by various feasible methods are still much too high to permit large-scale application. However, for human consumption in a few high cost places demineralized water is already being produced. By and large future requirements can probably be met in most areas of the world provided necessary investments are made and water is used with increasing efficiency.

CONCLUDING OBSERVATIONS

We have tried to marshal what statistical evidence we could readily find to shed light on the important question: are resources becoming scarcer in the United States and the world? The picture that emerges is not simple and clearcut. Limiting our forward look to the year 2000, we find no general increase in scarcity in the more developed areas; the opposite trend is likely to continue. In the less developed areas severe problems will be encountered, but the situation is not hopeless. Much will depend on policies both in the aid-receiving and the aid-giving countries, and on the international economic and political climate generally. Most important will be the effort put forth and the competence of people in those countries in dealing with their resource problems and potentialities.

For the United States, historical data have been assembled and systematic projections have been made to the year 2000. The U. S. historical data do not point to increasing scarcity in any general sense. Indications as to future technology and supply possibilities, when matched against projected demand for the next four decades, likewise do not indicate a general tendency toward increase in scarcity. A continued rise in the level of living seems assured. This does not mean there will not be supply problems for particular resources at particular times and places; rather it means that in this country technologic and economic progress, building upon an ample and diversified resource and industrial base, gives assurance that supply problems can be met. If this rather favorable prognosis is to be guaranteed in fact, scientific and technologic advance will have to continue unabated and the results will have to be translated into economic reality. In addition, it will be essential to extend, or at least maintain to the present degree, a world trading and investing system in which raw material deficits can be met through imports from other countries with a surplus of these materials. Any devastating war would, of course, throw off all of the projections undertaken in this paper as well as conclusions drawn from them.

The historical data for most of the world, particularly the less developed areas, are not extensive or reliable enough to support more than highly tentative conclusions regarding long range future adequacy of natural resources and raw materials. We have examined such evidence as we could readily find. For the more developed countries, particularly in Western Europe, where the data are reasonably good, the trend is not unlike that for the United States, according to the historical evidence and the projections we have made. The importance of a viable world trading system is, if anything, greater for the other more developed economies since they tend to rely more heavily on raw material imports and upon exports of processed goods in exchange for them. The success of the European Common Market and the European Coal and Steel Community over recent years is an indication of the importance of widening the area of freer trade.

In the less developed areas of the world, the data are extremely thin and projections hazardous. One simply does not know enough about historical trends to gauge the rapidity with which technical advances already made in the more developed countries will be applied widely in the less developed ones. Nor can population projections be relied upon as coming very close to what will actually happen.

Nevertheless, we have speculated on possibilities of future resource demand and supply in the less developed countries in the preceding two sections of this paper. We are not persuaded that the next few decades will see any general and marked deterioration of living levels because of increasing scarcity of raw materials. On the other hand, prospective rates of population increase are high in many countries and do not afford much assurance that living levels can be increased very rapidly. We are willing to venture the tentative view that living levels in most of the less developed countries can and probably will increase over the coming years with diets improving quite slowly and energy and mineral use more rapidly. It is quite possible, of course, that food consumption would increase more rapidly if population grew less rapidly. Whether these economies will be able to achieve a "take-off" into widespread industrialization and whether this will be translated promptly into substantial gains in levels of living are for the future to decide. We are inclined to think there is a good prospect of this happening in a number of places. The process depends most on education, motivation, and favorable policies and social adaptations. We do not believe that shortages and inadequacies of natural resources and raw materials are likely to make the more favorable outcomes impossible of achievement.

For the Soviet Union and the bloc countries of Eastern Europe, taken as a whole, continued and rapid economic growth should not be hampered by any lack of nautral resources. Large amounts of oil have recently been discovered and most minerals seem plentiful. Agriculture seems more uncertain, partly because of the natural difficulties and partly for institutional reasons. We attempt no generalization regarding Communist China.

There are certain escape hatches from any tendency toward increasing scarcity, and it is important that these be kept open. In fact, the challenge of public policy and private management of resource enterprises is to keep them open, both in developed and less developed countries. Among the escape hatches are the following:

1. Possibilities for substitution of a more plentiful, convenient, and cheaper material for one that is becoming scarcer (that is, rising in cost and price) will usually exist. The more diversified a country's technology, industry, and labor force, the more readily substitutions can be made. For example, in the United States over the past forty years there have been massive substitutions among building materials, metal alloys, foods, fuels, and many other categories of consumer and producer goods. Sometimes the impulse toward substitution arises from raw material level, perhaps because of the discovery of a new source; sometimes it arises at the final consumer end as when a family decides to switch from coal to gas heating; and sometimes a change at an intermediate level of processing triggers the substitution, for example, in the use of oxygen for steel making. In each case the implication for the resource materials may be considerable; some of the changes may be resource-saving and some resource-using, frequently saving for a scarcer resource and using for a more plentiful one.

2. An escape hatch of increasing importance in the resource field is the application of more than one use to a given basic resource such as land or water. The large economies and benefits to be secured from the multiple purpose development and use of a river system have long been well established, and now are being realized in development programs in many less developed countries. Use of water for irrigation, flood control, navigation, and hydroelectric power is now being combined with "new" purposes such as outdoor recreation, dilution of pollutants, and new industrial processes. Similarly, for land it will be increasingly desirable to develop and manage large tracts for multiple purposes of forest products production, animal grazing, agriculture, outdoor recreation, and planned urban development.

3. Yet another escape hatch, at least when the matter is viewed from the point of view of a particular country, is the importing of needed or cheaper raw materials from elsewhere. The United States in about 1930 shifted from being a net exporter of resource materials to a position of net importer, where it has remained ever since. This country is still a large exporter of wheat, cotton, and certain other raw materials, principally agricultural, and a net importer of crude oil, iron ore, copper, lead, zinc,

bauxite, and many mineral raw materials. Many of the less developed countries depend heavily upon exports of mineral and agricultural raw materials, and imports of yet other resource products. Increasingly most countries of the world will find it advantageous to their own development if a viable world trading and investment system can be maintained so that high cost programs of national sufficiency and autarchy will not be necessary. The more effectively such a system operates, the more productive the whole world economy will be, and the more chance there will be that tendency toward shortage can be eliminated or diffused over the world instead of becoming concentrated in particular countries.

4. Programs of resource research, conservation, development, and better management can also contribute to the avoidance of incipient tendencies toward scarcity. Frequently these need to be planned and integrated for particular regions. For example, in West Pakistan the better management of water used in agriculture could greatly increase yields and hence levels of food consumption. This assumes a variety of supporting investment activities as well as those directly focused upon agricultural land and water. Investment in land drainage and desalinization would be required in this case along with the application of more and better fertilizers, and improved systems of extension services, plus many other changes.

In some instances public and private policies of conservation (that is shifting the rate of use of the resource from the present toward the future) will be desirable as a part of national and regional development programs. For example, in selected instances the postponement of timber cutting or the catching of fish until the stock and growth rates are at more favorable levels will be helpful. Conservation in the sense of reduction of waste at various stages between initial development of the resource and final consumption of its products frequently will prove to be economical and can make an important contribution to the avoidance of shortage.

Resources research and development programs will have to be pursued vigorously if new sources of resource materials are to be found and cheaper substitutes are to be forthcoming. Without sufficient research and development, any optimism about the future would quickly vanish; with effective research and development, even stubborn problems can be made to yield.

It can be seen from these various observations regarding the central question of whether resources are becoming scarcer that much of the answer will lie outside the resource industries and activities themselves. General programs of education and more specialized programs for training scientists, technical personnel, and managers will be important. The capacity of people in less developed countries to make use of technologic improvements already successfully demonstrated in more developed areas will be of particular importance. Social organization and willingness to

experiment with new policies frequently will determine whether or not
a country will be successful in its development and use of natural resources. Land tenure arrangements, laws and customs regarding the ownership and use of water, willingness to try out new agricultural and forest
management techniques, and the like are of great significance. Institutions which make possible rapid transfer of knowledge and technique
from more to less developed areas should be given special attention. Extension service activities will be of critical importance.

It would appear desirable to initiate and maintain on a world scale
a continuing estimate of growing demand for resources and raw materials,
a continuing inventory of reserves and potential supplies at various levels
of cost, and an indicated matching of demands and supplies as a result of
various policies and actions.[19]

A final observation: further investigation of past resource development and use trends will make it possible to project future situations
more accurately. This chapter has attempted to bring together some of
the more significant and readily available resource data as a basis for
demand and supply projections for various major areas of the world. As
more work is done along these lines, it should be possible to specify more
clearly the emerging problem of scarcity so that farsighted policies can be
installed well in advance of the onset of desperate situations. As time goes
on, we should be able to answer with less and less indecision the central
question of whether or not resources are becoming scarcer over the world.

---

[19] As a step in this direction, Resources For The Future, Inc. has recently initiated
a series of steps by which historical trends in the energy commodities will be examined
on a world scale as a basis for making some projections of likely demand several decades
into the future. In this connection the establishment of a world resource development
institute has been proposed, which among other things, could sponsor comprehensive
and systematic projections of resource demand and supply. See Fisher and Revelle,
Natural Resource Policies and Planning for Developing Countries, United Nations Conference on the Application of Science and Technology for the Benefit of Less Developed Areas, Geneva, 1963.

Frank W. Notestein, Dudley Kirk,
and Sheldon Segal

7

The Problem of Population Control

The previous chapters have posed the problems of population growth. Here we shall examine the prospects of controlling population growth through reduction of the birth rate. We can best approach this problem of population control by considering first the reduction in fertility that has taken place in the West. What were the forces that brought about that reduction, and are these applicable in other parts of the world?

FRANK W. NOTESTEIN *is President of the Population Council. He was formerly Professor of Demography and Director of the Office of Population Research, Princeton University; and served also as the first Director (Consultant-Director) of the Population Division of the Bureau of Social Affairs of the United Nations. He is a Past President of the Population Association of America, a member of the American Statistical Association, of the American Association for the Advancement of Science, and of the International Union for the Scientific Study of Population.*

DUDLEY KIRK *is Demographic Director of the Population Council. He served formerly on the faculty and as a research associate at the Office of Population Research at Princeton; and also as demographer and in various other posts in the State Department. He is a past President of the Population Association of America, a Fellow of the American Statistical Association and a member of the International Union for the Scientific Study of Population.*

SHELDON SEGAL *is Assistant Medical Director of the Population Council. He served formerly on the faculty of the State University of Iowa and is presently on the faculty of Columbia University. He is a member of the International Institute of Embryology, the American Eugenics Society, the Association for the Scientific Study of Sterility and the American Association for the Advancement of Science.*

THE BACKGROUND

Fertility and mortality in nineteenth century Europe

Western Europe in the nineteenth Century was the scene of increasing political order, agricultural innovations, the commercial and industrial revolution, and the growth of medical science. Together these produced a gradual but persistent decline in the death rate. At the same time, birth rates fluctuated in the middle and high 30's (expressed as the number of annual births per 1000 population). These rates are lower than the birth rates in most of the underdeveloped areas in the twentieth Century, because marriage was generally rather late and a substantial number of women remained unmarried. The century was a period of sustained but slow population growth in Europe, rarely exceeding one and one-half per cent a year in any country.

Beginning about 1875, fertility rates in Western Europe began a decline that continued through the late 1930's, by which time they produced very slow growth. (It should be noted that the decline of the birth rate in France began much earlier—probably in the eighteenth Century. The causes are not clear, but the trend probably reflects the early rise of rationality in the French population.) In many countries there was a postwar rebound in the birth rate, but this has largely subsided. Birth rates in Europe today generally exceed death rates, but only enough to perpetuate a rather slow rate of population increase.

An explanation of the decline in Europe's birth rates has been attempted along three different lines, related to changes in reproductive capacity, to the development of improved contraceptives, and to social and economic changes that encourage the small-family ideal—the last representing part of the complex process often referred to as "the demographic transition."

Changes in reproductive capacity

J. deCastro is the most recent exponent of the view that a change in reproductive capacity is responsible for the transition from high to low fertility. In "The Geography of Hunger," he sets up the hypothesis that improved diet may impair the ability to reproduce, since laboratory animals on high-protein diets have been shown to have litters of reduced size. He then correlates crude birth rates with caloric intake for nations around the world, and finds that the nations with the poorest diets have the highest birth rates. Hunger, he suggests, is the cause rather than the consequence of population pressure.

There are some obvious weaknesses in this reasoning. First, the litter

size of laboratory animals has no demonstrated relation to human reproductive performance. Even simple analogy, invalid though it is, might
suggest a relationship between litter size and twinning or multiple births
rather than total reproductive performance. Secondly, correlation is a
measure of association, not of causation. Finally, and most damaging of
all, deCastro neglects the pertinent evidence that negates his hypothesis.
Many studies of middle-class, well fed American, British, and Scandina-
vian wives have shown conclusively that, unless they practice contraception, they conceive at rates that would yield a marital fertility quite as
high as any in the poorest underdeveloped countries. If anything, well
nourished and healthy women are better, not poorer, reproducers than
impoverished and disease-ridden women.

There may or may not be differences in reproductive capacity from
country to country. If such differences exist their effect on birth rates is
obscured by the large effects of differing social customs, and especially by
the prevalence and effectiveness of voluntary restrictions of births.

The development of improved contraceptives

The second theory attempts to explain the decline of fertility in
Western Europe as a result of the invention of effective contraceptive
methods, particularly the condom and the diaphragm. The theory has
been supported by Henry Pratt Fairchild and William F. Ogburn, among
others, and was suggested by the decline in the British birth rate that
followed the Bradlaugh-Besant trial in 1877—an event that gave great
publicity to practical birth control methods.

The theory fits many of the known facts. Birth rates began to decline first in the upper classes and in the urban centers, where information about the new inventions would spread most rapidly. It seeped
gradually down through the social strata and spread from industrialized
northwestern Europe to the agricultural southeast. Once effective contraceptive methods are known to all sectors of society, one would expect that
fertility would tend to be lowest among those who could least afford large
families. There is some evidence, notably in Stockholm, that fertility and
economic status were directly associated. A good case can, therefore, be
made for the view that the invention of better birth control methods was
a critical factor in the onset of the fertility decline.

There is one outstanding exception. In Ireland the crude birth rate
declined in much the same way as in other parts of the modern world,
but the fertility of married women remained as high as one would expect in the absence of contraceptive practice. The decline in Ireland was
the result of the growing proportion of spinsters and the advancing age of
marriage. With this exception, it has been fully demonstrated in all other
parts of the world where investigations of such matters have been made

that the major factor in the reduction of birth rates was the rapid spread and growing effectiveness of contraceptive practice, together with some increase in abortion.

Although the importance of contraceptive practice cannot be denied, there is one serious obstacle to an explanation of the modern reduction of fertility in terms of the invention of improved contraceptive methods. A wide range of studies during the last twenty-five years in the United States, Great Britain, and Scandinavia have shown that large sectors of the population are controlling their fertility without recourse to modern contraceptives. Millions of couples are successfully practicing *coitus interruptus* to control fertility. This method has been known for thousands of years, and used to some extent by all the major peoples of the world. There is substantial evidence that *coitus interruptus* began to be widely practiced in Europe when birth rates began to fall. The failure of birth rates to fall in other parts of the world clearly turns less on lack of effective means than on the absence of strong motivation.

The demographic transition in Europe

An appreciation of the motivational problem is easily gained if we consider the situation of mankind up to a moment ago in history. The problem has always been survival, not rapid population growth. We have no reason to suppose that any child born more than two centuries ago had an even chance of living as long as thirty years. In the face of heavy depletion by death, high fertility was a requirement for survival. The populations that have survived to inhabit the world's major regions all entered the modern era with the physiological capacity to reproduce abundantly, and with social institutions that fostered high birth rates.

There is great variety in the detailed forms in which the world's societies evolved to meet the challenge of survival, but the goal of high fertility is universally evident in the forms of economic organization, marital and familial institutions, educational systems, religious beliefs, means of gaining status, and even the informal sanctions of gossip and slander. There were few alternatives to early marriage and continuous childbearing as a means of livelihood or a sense of fulfilment for women. In the rather static self-sufficient peasant societies there was fairly little social mobility. Parents generally aspired to have their children "become their stations in life" rather than rise in the world. Individuals found their social position largely in terms of their parentage. Parents desired large families both as a labor force and as a guarantee, in days of uncontrolled mortality, that there would be surviving children to care for them in their old age. In short, the prevalent ideals emphasized the perpetuation of the family and the importance of large numbers of children.

The technological revolution brought changes that made the old ideals obsolete. In the burgeoning cities, neighbors knew little of each other's antecedents. What a man could do and what he possessed became more important for his status in life than his familial origin. Education became common. New occupations developed, offering new channels for advancement. Mortality came under progressive control, so that many children were no longer necessary to assure a few survivors who could care for the aged parents. Under such conditions a new set of standards gradually began to emerge. People began to want fewer children, to whom they could give better opportunities for health, education, and advancement. The practice of birth control became more widespread and more effective, and birth rates gradually began to fall.

On the other hand, people have always sought to avoid illness and postpone death by any means. Witchcraft, incantation, prayer, and pre-modern medicine all had very limited success, but the end was highly desired and all available means continued to be used, regardless of their efficacy. As soon as effective means of controlling disease became available, death rates declined.

The decline of the birth rate came more slowly, pending the obsolescence of ancient values centered on the perpetuation of the extended family group, and the emergence in the modern setting of new values centering on the welfare and opportunities of the nuclear family. As the new ideals began to emerge, the population began the extensive practice of birth control. It is the lagging decline of the birth rate behind the death rate that accounts for the major part of the modern epoch of population growth.

This account of the "demographic transition" in the West is over-simplified, but it is essentially correct. Technological modernization almost inevitably entails transitional population growth, because the reduction of mortality requires only effective means, whereas the reduction of fertility involves questions of both means and ends.

Demographic prospects in developing countries

It should be noted that Europe was fortunate in the circumstances of its demographic transition. There was room for increase in numbers—Europe itself was rather lightly populated at the beginning of the modern era, and there was more than enough room for expansion in the New World. The control of mortality was being learned only gradually, and the decline of death rates was slow. In historical terms population growth was rapid, but in the light of trends in the underdeveloped countries in the mid-twentieth century the growth of Europe's population was relatively slow. Still the transition from a system that had maintained the population on the basis of high birth rates balanced by high death rates, to the modern system that maintains it on the basis of low birth and death rates, involved a three-fold increase in Europe, and a five- to seven-fold increase of European populations throughout the world.

The nations undergoing modernization in the twentieth century face an entirely different situation. Thanks to the efficiency of the pre-modern rice culture, many of the Asian nations enter the period of modernization with relatively dense populations. We have become marvelously efficient in the control of disease—at the comparable stage of development in nineteenth-century Europe, death rates were dropping only one third to one fifth as fast. Today some of the lowest death rates in the world are to be found in the underdeveloped areas where public health protection is relatively advanced, as in Ceylon, Singapore, and Taiwan. In its period of modernization Europe faced annual rates of growth of one per cent or less. Today two per cent is general, and many countries are growing at from three to three and one half per cent annually. Some appreciation of the difficulties that these rates impose in terms of economic drain may be obained from the fact that one per cent doubles a population in sixty-nine years, whereas an annual increase of three and one half per cent doubles it in about twenty years. Moreover, the newly modernizing countries have no space for expansion such as the New World afforded Europe during its epoch of modernization.

Such a description of the difficulties now faced occasionally elicits the response that it represents a purely arithmetic prediction. Demographers have been wrong before and doubtless they will be wrong again. But our fallibility offers no reassurance. We cannot be certain the populations will grow, but we are certain that, if birth rates remain unchanged, only a catastrophic rise in death rates will prevent growth. Such a rise in mortality would demonstrate the bankruptcy of all our efforts. No one, least of all the people involved, can look forward to a rising death rate as a desirable mode of escape from the problems of population growth. Those who advocate letting the birth rate take its natural course may indeed be implicitly fostering a resurgent death rate and the failure of our efforts at modernization.

THE PROBLEM

The necessity of population control

If we value life and health, education, and relief from poverty, the need for an early reduction of the birth rate is acute. Birth rates in the past have fallen most rapidly in the context of modernization and social-economic change. But there is nothing in the European experience to suggest that we must rely on gradual and automatic changes in society. One often meets the glib generalizations, particularly in the underdeveloped countries, that it is only necessary to concentrate on economic modernization, since it is well known that we can rely on these processes to bring the birth rate down automatically. The argument completely neglects the means—for example, the role that the most objectionable and dangerous forms of abortion might play in the absence of more humane methods, and the train of suffering such developments entail. Perhaps even more important, it neglects entirely the time-span required for such an adjustment, and the tragic consequences that may follow to the entire society if the trend does not come rapidly enough.

There is every reason to believe that the process of reducing the birth rate can be greatly accelerated. We shall return to the question of ways and means when we come to an appraisal of future prospects. But first it may be useful to consider what influence the world's various religions may have on the possibilities of spreading the practice of family planning.

Religion and population control

As a matter of doctrine, Moslems, Hindus, Buddhists, and Confucianists have no generally accepted or firmly administered opposition to birth control. Distinguished representatives of each can be found with all shades of opinion, but none is in a position to carry dominant sections of the laity with him. Moreover, recent governmental pronouncements favorable to the control of fertility have helped to give weight to the leaders who favor birth control.

The Roman Catholic position presents the only major theological obstacle to population control. The Catholic position does not concern population growth, but individual obligations for procreation and parental responsibility. Within that framework, constraints relate entirely to means by which fertility is regulated. Thus far it is not clear that the Church will sanction any method of regulation other than total abstinence or abstinence during the fertile part of the menstrual cycle. The position relating to medication that "regulates the cycle" or blocks ovulation has not been fully elaborated.

From an exterior point of view the Roman position embodies certain advantages for the future regulation of fertility. It is so tightly drawn and carefully elaborated that, as an obstacle to the limitation of fertility, it is vulnerable to circumvention by advances in scientific knowledge. If we should learn how to forecast ovulation within forty-eight hours, fertility could be "licitly" controlled by abstention for only two days a month. Needless to say, such knowledge would have importance in the solution of the problems of population growth far beyond the confines of the Catholic group.

The major difficulty with the Catholic position, from the point of view of fostering the spread of family planning, lies less in the substantial impact of that position on its own adherents than on the Church's political influence. Fear that a soft position will foster the use of methods it opposes has led the Church's adherents to be very cautious about supporting international programs of technical aid for countries seeking help for their birth control programs, and to advocate legal constraints to such practices by Catholics and non-Catholics alike. There is, however, some indication that efforts of this kind are being reduced.

The major influence of religion on reproductive behavior often lies outside the strictly theological field. It lies in the changes of the way of life which the religious tend to impede—for example, the rising status of women, aspirations for social mobility, the values attaching to secular education, and the like. In Europe such matters have not greatly differentiated Catholic and non-Catholic. Today it is noteworthy that birth rates are lower in Belgium, France, Italy, Spain, and Portugal than they are in the United States. The methods used to attain such regulation are not well known. Undoubtedly they are partly "licit" but partly "illicit" from the Catholic point of view. By contrast the highest fertility for any major region of the world is found in "Catholic" Latin America. Thus the behavior of Catholic populations runs the gamut of world-wide experience and reflects chiefly the varying cultural background of its adherents.

The same can be said of the other major religions. To the extent that all religions tend to perpetuate traditional modes of behavior, they are of course obstacles to change. In this they are not essentially different from other institutionalized aspects of the value system—for example, the political and economic structures, and the familial organization. In all aspects of social life the detailed arrangements that foster fundamental goals have developed in the historical setting. This fact is not to be regretted, for it is doubtful that man could survive without the binding cement of non-rational loyalty to traditional goals, of which those relating to religion represent only a part. The difficulty is that means of attaining fundamental goals, which were effective in the past, may become obstacles to their attainment in new and radically different settings. The problem of education, whether in the political, economic, social, or religious field, is not a problem of shifting fundamental and universal human values, but rather of fostering the growth of appropriate means for their attainment in a new setting. It requires delicacy of timing and the wisdom that avoids loss of orientation, while permitting sufficiently rapid change to meet the requirements of accelerating technological development. These two-fold needs have many manifestations, but in the field of birth control they imply the necessity for educational efforts stressing such fundamental values—the welfare of the nuclear family, the protection of motherhood, the responsibility of parenthood, the health and educational opportunities of children, and the dignity of individual life.

Programs of population control

Social inertia is undoubtedly an obstacle to the rapid spread of family planning. But it is not an insuperable obstacle, as is sometimes inferred from the fact that no governmental programs have thus far been effective in reducing the birth rate. The inference is false. Until eight years ago no government had even begun to elaborate a national program, and no serious effort has been in effect for even so short a period as five years.

If family planning is to spread in the underdeveloped regions it will require substantial and well-organized programs. The effort will have to be consolidated with the newly developing health, communication, and community development services of the nation. It requires large cadres of paramedical personnel to reach the villages, and a well-trained supervisory force to administer the programs. It requires national institutions to set standards and maintain them, to train personnel, and to develop such educational materials as film strips, posters, leaflets, and the like. In short, national family planning programs will have to draw on all the instrumentalities of adult education. At present there are few institutions in either the underdeveloped or the advanced countries able to supply the necessary developmental work and training. They must be built. Fortunately both here and abroad some public health institutions are beginning to move in this direction.

Analogous efforts have been made in agricultural extension, public health, and public administration. These efforts have drawn on a large fund of experience with problems that are similar throughout the world. The case of birth control is more difficult because there have been very few efforts to mount national programs; for lack of experience we do not know how to be truly efficient in our approach.

This fact dictates the necessity of research. While the major institutions and programs are being built, there must be a range of field trials designed to test the suitability and efficiency of a wide variety of approaches and of materials. We cannot afford to be wasteful, for the problems are huge and available resources are scarce. It will be necessary to run pilot tests of all procedures before they are adopted on a national scale. Organizational and instructional work can go ahead while this research is in progress. We can all learn while we are doing, and quickly incorporate new knowledge into the general programs. Such efforts are being undertaken in the United States, India, Pakistan, Ceylon, Taiwan, and a number of other areas—but only a beginning has been made.

If governmental programs to promote birth control have not been operating long enough to demonstrate their effectiveness, why then our confidence that they can become effective? It rests on two grounds, the first general, the second specific. In the first place educational programs in many other fields have clearly been effective in modifying individual behavior. This is demonstrably true in agriculture, health, and religion. The same principles are involved in the case of birth control. In the second place, experimental successes have been obtained, notably in Singur outside Calcutta and by the Swedish mission to Ceylon. In both instances the trials were conducted in peasant populations. In Singur relatively untrained paramedical personnel, utilizing simple and inexpensive conventional means of birth control, have reduced the birth rate in the experimental area by about fifteen per cent in four years, while the birth rate in the control area remained unchanged. In Ceylon, in a somewhat more literate population, and with a more concentrated effort, the Swedish experiment has reduced the birth rate of the experimental villages by about one third. Results that can be obtained in experimental programs can be duplicated on a wider scale, given the necessary organizational effort.

Sometimes there is a disposition to delay the entire effort until scientific advances give more effective, cheaper, and more acceptable methods. The suggestion is dangerous. The work of training, organization, and pilot testing takes time. It can be undertaken effectively now with methods that are already available. If the educational and organizationl work is not done, any new discovery will make small difference in the immediate future, since without the preliminary work it cannot be brought to the people.

Heavy and repeated emphasis has been laid on the problems of motivation and education because they are too often neglected. It is clear, however, that means are also important. The difficulties of the motivational situation only underscore the need for a wide range of effective, cheap, and esthetically and morally acceptable methods to meet requirements in different parts of the world. Little research was formerly devoted to either the scientific or the technological aspects of fertility control. Fortunately, this situation is beginning to change and the prospects for future developments are excellent.

PHYSIOLOGIC FERTILITY CONTROL

The physiologic control of fertility includes enhancement as well as suppression of fertility. For many years the major incentive for research in reproduction was the problem of infertility. More recently the emphasis has shifted, and there has been increased awareness by scientists of the importance of providing new means to restrict fertility when desired.

No single method of fertility limitation may be expected to satisfy the diverse needs of the world's expanding populations. An effective method may be perfectly acceptable in one society and completely useless in another part of the world, for reasons of culture, religion, environmental conditions, or because of physiologic differences. Even a single country's contraceptive needs are varied. It becomes essential, therefore, to consider research in contraception not as a search for "the pill" or "the inoculation" but as an effort to find several acceptable means based on a variety of action mechanisms.

Research has shown that there are several steps in the reproductive process which may be vulnerable to controlled interference and could thus provide means for the voluntary regulation of fertility. Some entirely new contraceptive methods have resulted from work along these lines.

Suppression of ovulation

The most advanced work centers upon the process of ovulation. Endocrinologists established that this key event occurs only when the ovary is influenced by gonad-stimulating hormones from the pituitary gland. Thus inhibition of these hormones could have the secondary effect of preventing the monthly release of eggs.

Steroid hormones produced by the male and female sex glands can cause this inhibition but, as a practical method of ovulation suppression, the administration of these substances presents serious disadvantages. Androgen, the male sex hormone, produces virilization in many women when doses sufficient to inhibit ovulation are given. Estrogen, the female sex hormone, tends to produce irregular and abnormal menstrual bleeding. The other sex hormone, progesterone, is at best a weak suppressor of pituitary gonadotrophins. Particularly when administered orally, large doses are required and effectiveness is less than complete.

At about the same time that investigations had suggested the utility of oral progesterone in combination with small amounts of estrogen, steroid chemists synthesized a series of compounds that proved to have effects on the reproductive system similar to the proposed combination. These analogues of the steroid hormones were developed for their potential utility as cancer chemotherapeutics, as anabolic agents in the field of geriatrics and, paradoxically, in the belief that their activity would be applicable in the treatment of some types of female sterility and habitual abortion.

As it turned out, the synthetic steroid hormones, which are characterized as *oral progestins,* were found to have the dual action of suppressing pituitary gonad-stimulating hormones and developing the uterine lining (endometrium) to a pre-menstrual condition, without the frequent occurrence of irregular bleeding. With these biologic effects it was possible to induce menstrual cycles in some women with long histories of amenorrhea and sterility. The compound was administered cyclically, twenty days each month. During this time the pituitary production of gonadotrophins was completely suppressed and the uterine lining developed to the pre-menstrual state. Upon withdrawal of therapy endometrial breakdown ensued, with menstrual bleeding; the induced cycle could then be repeated.

This experience showed that steroid-induced pituitary suppression and ovulation inhibition could be achieved without the untoward contraindications of the naturally produced steroid sex hormones. The stage was set for contraceptive trials of the new compounds, and the results indicated remarkable success. In 1956 a field trial of an oral progestin as a contraceptive was initiated in Puerto Rico. By 1963 over 10,000 women in the United States, Britain, Mexico, Japan, and elsewhere were involved in carefully recorded trials of nearly a score of related compounds; over 50,000 woman-years of exposure are compiled in the documented reports of these studies. Probably no single class of drugs ever before received such wide distribution in clinical trials before being introduced for public use.

This episode in modern medicine was marked by enthusiasm in some quarters, caution in others, and alarm, religious controversy, appraisal and re-appraisal in the world-wide medical and lay press. The contraceptive effectiveness of the method was never in doubt. Some studies demonstrated one hundred per cent protection against pregnancy when the pill-taking schedule was followed as prescribed. Most of the discussion regarding usefulness of the method centered on cost, side effects, complexity of dosage schedule, and the possibilities of long-range effects. The most serious question raised was the suggestion in 1962 that the oral progestins may increase the chances of thrombophlebitis or an even more catastrophic blood-clotting episode. Thromboembolism was diagnosed in a number of women who were using an oral progestin for contraception or for the treatment of a gynecological disorder. However, by this time nearly two million women had used the drug, and it is impossible to establish whether or not the reported cases of thromboembolic disease represent a higher incidence than would be expected in the general population.

In the use of oral progestins for contraception, the most frequent problem encountered is the occurrence of transient side effects, such as nausea and irregular menstrual bleeding. Although these manifestations are usually limited to the first few cycles of therapy, they necessitate constant medical supervision. There is, therefore, considerable room for perfecting this method of contraception. The search for new compounds that minimize the need for medical supervision and simplify the schedule of drug administration remains an important research undertaking.

Chemical suppression of sperm production

The testis, like the ovary, depends upon stimulation by pituitary gonadotrophic hormones in order to perform its normal function of producing sex hormones and sperm. Like the ovary, the testis can be secondarily suppressed by a procedure that stops the production of gonadotrophins. The oral progestins, for example, could be effective agents for the inhibition of sperm production. At the same time, however, they have the unwelcome effect of inhibiting the secretion of sex hormones by the testis; as a consequence, potency and libido are markedly reduced.

There are other orally active chemical compounds that halt sperm production without interfering with testicular hormone secretion. Several classes of chemical substances have been found to have this effect, but all have accompanying side effects that render them unsatisfactory for contraceptive purposes. One group of such compounds is the nitrofurans, which have had wide use as inhibitors of bacterial growth. They are very effective in stopping sperm production in man, but the doses required cause nausea and headache. In 1960 great promise was seen in another group of compounds, originally of interest for their usefulness in the treatment of intestinal amoebae. The drugs were tested using volunteers among penitentiary prisoners; complete suppression of sperm count was demonstrable. When the drug was discontinued, sperm count returned to normal. With high hopes, trials were expanded to include men in more usual social circumstances. The first unexpected observation was that the drug enhanced the vascular effects of imbibed alcohol. As careful follow-up of the original prisoner-volunteers continued, it was suspected that the drugs could be causing liver damage. This of course discouraged further testing, and the drugs were withdrawn from clinical application. Subsequently, other compounds with anti-spermatogenic activity have been synthesized and promising laboratory results obtained. The discovery of an orally active compound with this type of effect, and free of harmful side effects, would provide an extremely useful method of contraception.

Interference with post-ovulatory events

A promising development has been revival of scientific interest in intra-uterine contraception. This technique, as popularized in Germany in the 1920's, involved the insertion into the uterus of a small, flexible, silver ring. The foreign object could remain in place as long as contraception was desired. Gräfenberg, the gynecologist whose name is associated with the method, had done 600 insertions by 1930, and reported the extremely low failure rate of 1.6 per cent. As others attempted to use the method, however, there were reports of undesirable complications, and the procedure was viewed with disfavor by the medical profession. Nevertheless, intra-uterine contraception was not completely abandoned. In 1959 a report was published on more than nineteen thousand Japanese women who had had ring insertions over a twenty-year period. These observations confirmed the high contraceptive effectiveness and contributed the important fact that this large group of women experienced no serious complications. This and similar favorable reports from Israel and the United States stimulated new interest and gave impetus to the initiation of many clinical trials of a variety of intra-uterine devices.

The new work introduced two important advances, which may eliminate the hazards associated with the original metal rings. First, inert plastics, which do not cause tissue reactions, were adopted in place of silver; secondly, the need for cervical dilation, a minor surgical procedure, was eliminated by the use of a thin plastic tube which can easily be inserted into the cervix, and through which the device can be introduced into the uterus. By 1963 one of the largest studies included 1000 women with an accumulated exposure of 9000 months, or 750 woman-years of exposure to pregnancy. In a non-contracepting group of fertile women, one would expect at least 375 pregnancies in this period. In the study group only thirty pregnancies occurred. Furthermore, most of the thirty pregnancies occurred with the use of an early design, which was later replaced by a modified device intended to eliminate certain shortcomings. With the newer modification only one pregnancy occurred, so that the method was proven to be over 99.7 per cent effective—a remarkable result.

These studies offer no clue as to the physiologic mechanism involved in the action of intra-uterine devices. It is clear that they do not act as a mechanical barrier to sperm passage to the arena of fertilization. It is more likely that they alter in some fashion the synchrony of events necessary for successful fertilization, transport of the fertilized egg in the female duct system, and development of the endometrium in preparation for implantation of the egg. Better understanding of the mechanism will aid considerably in discovering the optimal type of device and in resolving such questions as when insertions should best be performed with relation to menses or a previous delivery.

The problems encountered with intra-uterine contraception include abnormal bleeding during the month after insertion, a few days of pain and discomfort in some women, and the involuntary extrusion of the device in a small percentage of cases. These difficulties are probably related to the size and shape of the object introduced into the uterus. Considerable research is needed to test modifications in design and material in order to develop trouble-free intra-uterine devices.

Procedures effective in laboratory animals

While research with oral progestins, anti-spermatogenic agents, and intra-uterine devices was progressing to the clinical stage, additional animal experimentation was going forward. This work focused upon several different links in the biologic chain of events involved in reproduction.

Immunologic approaches—Considerable emphasis was placed on developing an immunologic mechanism to interfere with the reproductive processes. This work envisaged the discovery of an inoculation that would impair fertility in a controlled fashion. Two approaches have proven successful in laboratory animals: the formation of antibodies against gonad-stimulating hormone and against spermatozoa. In each case a male or female animal undergoes a loss of fertility after a suitable series of inoculations. The effect is short-lived when antibodies to gonad-stimulating hormone are injected. There are still many problems involved in preparing pure and specific antibodies, however, so that possible human application depends upon further refinements. The use of antibodies against spermatozoa presents even greater complications. One of the most serious is how to achieve reversibility of the effect. This and other problems require experimentation and, in part, must attend further advances in the science of immunology.

Anti-zygote activity—The zygote, or newly fertilized egg in the earliest stages of development, spends several days passing through the female reproductive tract before it is ready to begin the process of implantation in the uterine lining. This period of zygote passage has been recognized as a highly vulnerable point in the reproductive process. Gynecologists believe that more than ten per cent of human fertilizations terminate because of degradation of the fertilized egg during this time, for some unexplained reason. Several synthetic compounds have been discovered, which cause zygote degradation when administered to rats shortly after fertilization has occurred. Assuming that the activity in the rat would carry over to the human, these drugs suggest another method of fertility control. Pills taken orally for a day or two after intercourse would prevent egg development if fertilization had occurred. There would be no disruption of the natural menstrual cycle and no manifestation whatever of the pregnant state. Indeed, there is no physiologic criterion by which any stage of the process could be classified as a pregnancy.

Chemical abortifacient agents—For many years the search for safe chemical abortifacient agents was directed toward finding drugs that would interfere with the development of the embryo and lead to an early abortion. Several were found, but their use proved to be extremely hazardous. Sub-optimal conditions of dosing could interfere with normal embryonic development without actual termination of pregnancy. Excessive doses could be very harmful to the mother. With increasing knowledge of how the placenta is formed and its biochemistry, the focus changed. Efforts were directed to finding ways to induce early abortion by chemical interference with mechanisms necessary for normal placenta formation and maintenance. It was established that early pregnancies in rats could be terminated at will by oral administration of substances that interfere with the biochemical requirements of the placenta. Further exploration of this field holds great promise not only for purposes of prevention, but for the development of means of protecting pregnancies in women who experience habitual spontaneous abortions.

PRACTICAL PROSPECTS

As the foregoing suggests, given the necessary research effort, the prospects for the development of new and more appropriate methods of limiting fertility are excellent. It is only essential that the work be pushed while the organizational, educational, and training programs go forward.

International cooperation in population control

In this connection a word should be said about the possibilities for technical aid by governments and international organizations to countries requesting such aid. Far too often the problem has been avoided on grounds of its political sensitivity. What we fail to realize is that a large portion of the costly and essential work of organization and training lies in areas that are not at all sensitive. Before any of the underdeveloped countries can effectively spread the practice of family limitation, they must have reasonably well-developed services in maternal and child health, health education, and community development. Work in these areas is not sensitive but does require a great deal of organization, training, and equipment. Once such work is established it will be much easier for the governments involved to introduce their own services in the field of birth control.

Occasionally one hears the objection that such efforts only complicate the problems of population growth by reducing the death rate. In the narrow sense it is true, but it is basically false. No efforts at social-economic development can be successful in a disease-ridden population, nor will a desire for small families be likely to emerge. Better health and improved chances for survival of the individual child lie at the root of the motivational change we are seeking. Frightened by the sensitive aspects of the subject, the world's governments and international agencies have seriously neglected the important kinds of assistance they can easily render.

The situation in developing countries

Where then do we stand? On the one hand there are many discouraging elements. The underdeveloped countries are extremely heavily populated for economies that depend on agriculture. The levels of income are low. The birth rates are higher than those of pre-modern Western Europe, although they are not higher than those of the United States about 1800, or of Russia in the early twentieth century. Population growth has been speeded by the efficiency with which contagions and infections are now controlled. Death rates have been dropping in the underdeveloped countries at a faster rate than seemed possible even twenty years ago. The rates of growth are now much higher than those of Europe while it was undergoing modernization and its demographic transition. The risks of failure in the efforts of development are very great unless today's underdeveloped countries can reduce their birth rates much more rapidly than Europe did. The problem could scarcely be more urgent, and it must be faced now and for at least the next two or three decades.

There are also hopeful factors. Europeans reduced their birth rates in the face of opposition by their governments and their religious and civic leaders. They did so because in the new setting of a modernized society the individual citizen took action in spite of the public position taken by his leaders.

Today we face a radically different situation. Government after government is coming to understand the urgency of the problem. The Japanese were the first non-European people to face the problem and to meet it with policies designed to facilitate population control. The Government of India enunciated a population policy in its first Five Year Plan, but began active organization only about 1956. It has devoted ever-increasing resources to spreading the practice of family planning. No large national impact was evident by 1963, nor could any be expected in such a short time. Just as the Western World had to do the innovating in the field of public health, India and other countries must learn how to tackle the problem of fertility regulation.

Pakistan adopted a similar governmental policy, with active organization of an extensive program backed by substantial budgets and some foreign technical aid from the Government of Sweden and American foundations.

Taiwan has no formal population policy, but the Provincial Government, with the aid of the Population Council of New York, is carrying on extensive experimental work of a highly promising character. Even before such work was organized there was clear evidence that fertility rates for women above age thirty were beginning to decline. The situation is far from typical because the population is essentially literate, has good health, and the constraints to growth of this island population are obvious to its inhabitants. Taiwan may indeed lead the underdeveloped areas of the Far East in the rapidity with which birth control spreads.

Singapore too has an active program, conducted by the local birth control organization with some subvention from the government. There also birth rates are beginning to fall. The governments of Korea, Turkey, and Egypt have announced programs furthering the spread of family planning. At a meeting of the United Nations General Assembly in late 1962 the major Asian countries and the Moslem countries of the Middle East all supported the idea that the United Nations provide technical assistance in this field.

These changed attitudes add a wholly new element to the situation.

No one knows how rapidly birth rates can be induced to decline if governments take a strong stand and implement their stand with effective programs. No one knows because it has never been tried for a sustained period. On theoretical grounds there is considerable reason for optimism, because the trend toward modernization is running very strong throughout the world.

To the driving force of governmental leadership, we must add the fact that the prospects are excellent for obtaining much more suitable methods than were formerly available. There are substantial reasons for optimism and there is no basis for the view that only tragic developments are possible. The answers will surely depend on the energy and resources with which the governments themselves approach the problem, and the vigor of technical support provided from the developed countries.

It should not be supposed that the foregoing optimistic view suggests that populations can be quickly stopped from growing, much less reduced in absolute numbers. The control of mortality is much too efficient and the age distributions are so heavily loaded with young people progressively moving into the reproductive years that substantial growth is inevitable. We can, however, hope for a very considerable curtailment of the rates of increase. On such a curtailment in a few decades depends much of the chances for modernization and escape from elemental poverty.

Frank Lorimer

8

Issues of Population Policy

POPULATION AS A WORLD PROBLEM

Questions of policy relative to population trends are, in large part, regional and specific. An attempt to treat the problems of the United States, Africa, France and Pakistan in the same terms is likely to promote confusion rather than enlightenment.

Yet the accelerated increase of mankind is having, and will have, (See Chapter 2) far-reaching consequences which can not be easily formulated but which profoundly affect the whole basis of human life and the structure of society.

"The present era is unique in that a predominance of man in the earthly environment is being established such as has never before existed." (United Nations, *The Future Growth of Population*, p. 21.) We are in the midst of an *ecological revolution*. This revolution is as irreversible as the leveling of mountains by rain and wind. It is due in part, though only in part, to the rapid proliferation of the human species. It affects the springs of water in the woods—with which many of our older citizens have been, but fewer of our younger citizens will be, familiar. It must also affect the springs of human experience and its expression in art, music, and poetry.

FRANK LORIMER *is professor of Sociology in the Graduate School of American University. He has had such important demographic assignments as: Technical Secretary to the Committee on Population Problems of the National Resources Committee; Consultant to the National Resources Planning Board; Consultant to the Office of Strategic Services; Chief, Economics Function section in the Foreign Economic Administration; Chief of the Population and Employment Branch of the Supreme Command, Allied Powers, Tokyo; and Research Associate of the Office of Population Research, Princeton University. He has served as administrative Director of the International Population Union. He is a past President of the International Union for the Scientific Study of Population and of the Population Association of America.*

The ecological revolution is changing the natural basis of human existence, society, and experience. It will bring good and evil of unforeseeable kinds and magnitudes. Is mankind spiritually prepared to deal appropriately with these revolutionary changes? Would it not be wise, if this were possible, to modify these trends so that our passage from the natural ecology in which human societies were formed into the uncharted, more "artificial" world of mass societies in constricted space may be less precipitous?

In a more immediate sense, trends which threaten the national aspirations of more than half the world's population present a problem to all nations. Frustration breeds envy, suspicion and violence. The security of the lucky nations with large natural resources, accumulated wealth and advanced techniques may be critically affected by the progress or reverses experienced in less fortunate nations during the next few decades.

Population questions are now an important issue in world affairs. This fact recently received explicit recognition in the approval by the United Nations General Assembly of a resolution on "Population Growth and Economic Development." We will comment at a later point on the positions of various governments on this resolution. Their statements reflect the deep concern of many governments on this subject, but also the strong resistance of others to any positive action in this field. It is now evident that issues relating to population are increasingly important in international affairs.

The development of American policies relating to population trends must, therefore, be framed in a world context.

OBSTACLES TO OBJECTIVE ANALYSIS

Much of the discussion on population questions is channeled through well-worn grooves to antagonistic positions. Each of the positions is characterized by over-simplification. The proponents of each position reinforce one another in their arguments and stimulate counter-attack by their opponents. This hampers objective analysis and a fresh approach to policy formation.

The confusion is, in part, a heritage of the century-and-a-half old Malthusian controversy. Malthus observed that population trends prior to his time were determined mainly by interaction between two primordial forces: the trend toward increase resulting from "the attraction between the sexes" and the "positive checks" of death and sterility due to hunger, disease, and vice. He assumed that production of the means of subsistence in any country, at a given stage of the slowly emerging arts, is largely determined by its natural resources. An advance of the arts releases a wave of population which soon absorbs the gains and reactivates the forces of misery. He held that the only way in which a nation can escape from perpetual poverty, due to the pressure of population on resources, is to restrict population growth by the exercise of prudential restraint. He did not comprehend the potentialities of science and technology, and his followers have persisted in minimizing their importance. They also minimize the importance of changes in social structure, culture and economic institutions. And, incidentally, they fix attention on absolute ratios of population to resources, as contrasted with the dynamic interrelation between demographic and economic changes, which may be more important over a considerable period than the absolute ratios.

Reactions to Malthusian dogma by proponents of changes in social institutions and by those concerned with the advancement of agriculture, the control of disease, etc., often lead them to an equally dogmatic denial of the economic and social effects of population trends.

A classic anti-Malthusian dogma was formulated by Karl Marx. The phenomenon described by Malthus as "over-population" is interpreted by Marxists as a "relative surplus" of labor. This is said to be an essential characteristic of capitalism, but non-existent in other types of society. The relation is stated as follows by T. V. Ryabushkin in "Social Aspects of Population Structure and Movement," United Nations: *World Population Conference, 1954* (Volume 5, meeting 28):

> Every social system has its own concrete laws of population. . . . In conditions of capitalistic mode of production a certain part of the population systematically becomes relatively superfluous. . . . In socialist society . . . the problem of excessive population no longer arises (pp. 1032-33). Thus the Malthusian theory is completely wrong and fruitless to explain historical facts. But maybe it has some sense for population policy in the future? Maybe it makes some sense to reduce rate of increase of population in any economically backward country in order to increase to some extent the level of well-being of population in the nearest future? To these questions we also give a sharp negative answer. *The Malthusian theory is harmful because it distracts attention from really scientific ways of increase of the working people's well-being.* (p. 1038, italics added.)

These dogmas present a false antithesis. They imply that the control of population and advances in economic productivity, health and education are *alternative* solutions to the problem of mass poverty. Most modern scientists, on the contrary, agree that they are essentially *complementary* and, in fact, mutually dependent.

There is considerable evidence that in the communist world anti-Malthusianism is more important as an ideological weapon than in actual conduct. Lenin, prior to the Russian revolution, had opposed the idea of a "birth-strike" against intolerable conditions of life in Germany as an expression of defeatism. However, he promoted contraception and abortion in the Soviet Union, allegedly on humanitarian grounds. This drastically reduced the economic burden of juvenile dependency in the early stages of socialist construction. (There were ten million fewer children in the USSR at the time of World War II than there would have been if fertility had remained at its early 1920 level.) It is unlikely that Lenin was completely indifferent to such effects. His program with respect to the control of births was reversed during the periods of forced collectivization and war when deaths exceeded births. It has subsequently been reestablished in the Soviet Union and in Eastern Europe. A similar ambivalence has been characteristic of Chinese policy in this field.

Opposition from other sources to concern about population trends often stems from a similar fear that attention to this topic may distract attention from other goals, such as the struggle against colonialism, the construction of giant industries, the improvement of a nation's health, reform of land tenure, or what not.

So the sterile controversy between Malthus and anti-Malthus goes on, fed and confused by extraneous issues. Liberals who demand freedom in personal affairs, social workers seeking to relieve the burdens of the poor, and isolationists who oppose American aid to improverished nations all seek support from neo-Malthusian theory. Opponents of contraception on religious grounds, radical politicians with Marxist leanings, and conservative statesmen, especially in the Latin countries of Western Europe, who view increase of population as a contribution to national power and prestige, ridicule "Anglo-Saxon Malthusianism."

There are other more subtle difficulties in an objective appraisal of population trends. Many of the words commonly used in demography are loaded with implicit values. An increase of population is the composite result of elements that are generally good in personal experience. In all societies, a birth is normally a "blessed event" whereas death is tragic. Positive evaluation of procreation and population growth is deeply rooted in the traditions of most societies. The very idea of "growth" generally has happy connotations; "bigger" has semantic associations with "better." Increases in crops, revenue, or population (though usually *not* increases in mental disease or in crime) are reported in official statistics as "gains"; decreases are reported as "losses," or "declines." Similarly, when a demographer writes about the number of births "needed" for the maintenance of a population, his readers and in some cases the demographer may unconsciously assume that this mathematical relation implies some sort of moral or social obligation.

These traditional loadings of descriptive terms with values that we tend to accept unconsciously are even more dangerous than the more obvious loading of words for forensic effect. The term "population explosion" is sometimes used quite innocently to point up the recent, unprecedented increase of population in the world. Yet the term connotes disaster. It was, in fact, introduced with this intent in a pamphlet originally entitled "The Population Bomb." Similarly, though with contrary intent, a scholarly Catholic writer in a recent book on family limitation refers to the decrease in the frequency of large families in the Western world as "incipient sterility," and to the increase in the proportions of aged persons as "premature sclerosis."

There is no sound basis for an *a priori* assumption that the increase or decrease of a population in any particular situation is either good or bad. The evaluation of actual or possible population trends is properly based on examination of their determinants and consequences in relation to accepted goals or values. Presumably no one would view with equanimity a trend toward the extinction of the human species, or of the nation of which he is a part. But any such fears today, with respect to mankind or to the United States, would be fantastic. The trend of the American people, which is now determined mainly by the preferences of potential parents, demonstrates that under normal conditions the spontaneous interests of individuals in marriage and parenthood assures the perpetuation of the human stock.

Under some conditions a temporary, or even a long-term, decrease of the population of an area or nation may be salutory. The sudden decrease of population in Ireland from about eight million in 1841 to 4.4 million in 1861, due to excess deaths and flight to other countries caused by the blight of the potato crop on which its economy depended, was the symptom rather than the cause of a catastrophe. Rapid increase of the Irish population during the previous century had intensified the crisis. Its subsequent gradual decrease through successive decades to about 2.8 million persons in 1960, due to delayed marriage, moderate fertility, and continued out-migration was a salutary adjustment to limited resources. Similarly, decreases of population in many rural countries and in the central cities of some metropolitan areas in the United States are normal accommodations to changing conditions.

It is our responsibility as citizens of this nation, and in a moral sense citizens of the world, to analyze population trends objectively and to study their determinants and consequences in relation to accepted social goals and human values. This task requires freedom from traditional dogmas, including academic dogmas, and from the tyranny of words. None of us can achieve complete freedom from prejudices, but we can put ourselves on guard against some of the latent pitfalls in current discussions on this subject.

DEMOGRAPHIC ASPECTS OF ECONOMIC AND SOCIAL DEVELOPMENT: GENERAL PRINCIPLES AFFECTING PUBLIC POLICY

Some issues of population policy are so complex that there is room for wide differences of opinion among sincere and intelligent persons on many points. This is conspicuously the case with respect to the relation between the general trend of population in the United States today and the trend of production. This relation is in net effect ambiguous—as indicated by the series of papers presented to a Conference on Demographic and Economic Change in Developed Countries, sponsored by the National Bureau of Economic Research (Princeton University Press, 1960). We will return to this topic at a later point.

On the other hand, some important principles concerning relations between population trends and economic and social conditions, particularly in underdeveloped countries, are clearly demonstrable, or can at least be acceptable as reasonable inferences from known facts. We will try to state some of these principles before moving to the consideration of more complex issues.

Rapid population increase hinders economic and social development in low-income countries today (See Chapters 3 and 4.)

Readers will note three reservations in this statement:

The term "hinders" does not necessarily imply blockage. Rapid increase of population is only one among many impediments to progress in the less developed countries, and the degree to which it is critically important varies widely among nations. Nevertheless, in countries where the force of other deterrent factors is nearly equal to the force of those favorable to a "take-off" in economic development, which is actually the case in many countries, an adverse population trend may block developmental programs and cause general disillusionment.

The statement is limited to countries with low income, which implies undeveloped technology.

Similarly the reference is to conditions "today." It excludes the historical question of the relation of population increase to economic and social advance in the former "new" lands of the modern world (e.g., early America or Australia) characteristized by (1) small population, (2) great unused resources, and (3) a cultural level comparable to that of the most advanced nations of the time with respect to literacy and capacity for discoveries and innovations. Under these conditions rapid population increase may have been a positive force in economic life, facilitating progress toward a balanced and diversified economy.

Economic and social advances along other lines facilitates the control of fertility

The conscious regulation of fertility depends primarily on personal motives. Under favorable conditions, governmental programs may influence the formation of popular attitudes in this field—in part merely by bringing the idea of controlling fertility without undue cost or personal strain into the consciousness of persons who have not previously thought of this as a real possibility. Governments may also influence behavior by providing more efficacious and/or more acceptable methods of controlling fertility. Officials, publicists, doctors and teachers may influence attitudes and behavior in other ways. Nevertheless, the question of personal motivation is always fundamental. (See Chapter 7.)

The effective control of fertility requires individual initiative and sustained effort. People who do not really believe that it is possible for them to improve conditions of life for themselves or their children will not undertake a radically new venture or put forth the sustained effort required for success in this undertaking. Where hope is weak, contraception will be absent or ineffective.

In any case, so long as children are, in an economic sense, capital assets that require relatively small investment and soon yield appreciable returns from their labor—as well as being objects of affection and a source of personal satisfaction and prestige—parents have no strong reason to limit the number of their offspring. The situation is changed radically by the introduction of new standards of child care and protection and, in particular, new educational opportunities and ambitions.

Furthermore, at a time when two-thirds of the infants born alive were likely to die before reaching maturity, only a moderately large family gave assurance against childlessness in old age—especially in societies where parental ambitions are focused exclusively on males. The reduction of infant mortality removes one of the strong motivations for unlimited procreation. Associated practices and values, such as attendance at clinics, the use of scientific medicine, and interest in hygiene and nutrition, are also conducive to the formation of rational attitudes favorable to effective family limitation.

Conversely, the formation of rational ideals concerning parenthood and the use of modern methods to regulate fertility favor the formation of progressive goals and the adoption of new techniques in agriculture, the treatment of disease, etc.

The most conspicuous decreases in annual birth rates (i.e., decreases of six points or more) during the postwar period occurred in the following countries (citing only those with fairly reliable statistics), according to *Population Index*, July, 1962:

	Birth Rates per 1,000 Population	
Country	Period ending 12/31/1949	1961
Japan	31.5	16.8
Singapore	46.4	35.5
Bulgaria	24.6	17.8[1]
Czechoslovakia	23.2	15.9
Hungary	20.8	14.0
Poland	28.4	20.7
Rumania	24.0	17.5
Yugoslavia	29.0	22.6
Finland	27.4	18.4
Puerto Rico	40.8	31.0

[1] 1960. Projection of the trend suggests the probability of a lower rate in 1961.

All the countries in this list are characterized (1) by official promotion, or at least toleration, of family limitation practices and (2) by significant progress in technology, health services and education. The downward movement of birth rates in Eastern Europe may be interpreted simply as a trend toward levels already established in Western Europe, but it was probably intensified in some cases, notably in Hungary, by special strains.

The extraordinary and drastic reduction of births in Japan has attracted world-wide attention. We call attention here to two aspects of this phenomenon. (1) Though continuous in important respects with pre-modern Japanese culture, the movement toward the control of fertility has been part of a general trend toward the rationalization and modernization of the Japanese economy. (2) In contrast to Europe where the spread of family planning was a purely popular and, in a sense, "subversive" movement, the Japanese movement was sponsored and encouraged by authoritative leadership in many fields: government, finance, schools, clinics, and the press.

The decrease of the birth rate in Puerto Rico is due in large part to the movement of young adults to the mainland. The movement toward planned parenthood in the island is associated with economic and social advances under the leadership of the Popular Party.

Well-planned and actively promoted family limitation programs sponsored by national governments, in conjunction with other progressive measures, can be expected to achieve significant results.

Empirical support for this statement is more tenuous than for the preceding propositions. It is not clearly demonstrable, but is asserted as a reasonable working hypothesis. (See Chapter 7.)

No well-informed person supposes that such a program could have an immediate effect on a large scale in the dispersed village population of a nation such as India. It has always required a considerable time for a family limitation movement in any country to gain momentum. Moreover, in the case of an official program it is important at first to focus attention mainly on experimental studies of the most effective and acceptable methods of controlling births in particular situations (among methods already at hand or others that may soon be made available) and on problems of organization and communication. Some pilot projects in rural India have yielded only negative results, but in some other cases the results are positive and encouraging. It has been found that the cooperation of respected leaders in community affairs is important in evoking a positive response in some situations.

The development of a family limitation movement in a low-income country with a large illiterate population is analogous in some ways to the promotion of major advances in agriculture, or the formation of an effective system of national defense. Such affairs can not be accomplished by simple legislative *fiat* and a few limited ventures. They require scientific research, systematic programming, and considerable investments of resources and energies.

The efficacy of national programs aimed at the reduction of fertility in low-income countries can be appreciably increased by external financial and technical assistance.

Family limitation programs have been inaugurated by the governments concerned, or proposed by the heads of government, in India, Pakistan, Ceylon, Singapore, Korea, Malaya, Tunisia, and the United Arab Republic. All of these governments are confronted with great needs and problems. Even though their leading statesmen recognize the urgency of their population problems and encounter little active opposition, it is difficult to provide the resources needed for the effective and expeditious development of such programs. (See Chapter 7.)

It is, of course, understood that external financial aid for this purpose would be extended only at the request of the governments concerned. It is also understood that expatriate technical assistants enlisted for service in this field would cooperate closely with the national governments, indigenous scientific institutes and educational institutions, and local leaders.

Finally, it is important to recognize that in many of the situations under consideration "time is of the essence." A program that in one decade might have enormous importance for the future prospects of a nation may be "too little and too late" a decade hence.

Discoveries in biological research may strongly affect future population trends.

There is a wide range of potential but still undeveloped methods of controlling fertility more simply and effectively. The results of experimental work in this field to date give large promise, and many interesting leads have as yet been only partially explored. The importance of research in this field with respect to population problems may be compared with the importance of atomic research in military affairs.

It is a matter of urgent importance that research on human reproduction be carried forward with all possible speed and that it include investigations in a wide range of related scientific fields. (See Chapter 7.)

CULTURAL CONFLICTS AFFECTING POPULATION POLICY

Background: The trend toward family limitation

The advance of technology brings social changes in its train. The growth of cities, electric communication, motor transportation, and medical science change people's ways of acting and thinking throughout the world, though the changes to date in some regions are relatively superficial. One of the normal consequences of technical change is a new interest in formal education. Another is a trend toward the purposive regulation of births. Many of these trends may be long delayed in some regions, with advances along some lines and lags in others. (See Chapter 7.) A critical issue emerges with respect to rates of change along different lines, and their coordination and interaction—with the possibility that lag in some fields may block the whole developmental process. (See Chapter 3.)

The purposive regulation of fertility is now firmly established and approaching universality in Europe, the Soviet Union, Japan, the United States, Australia and New Zealand. The gap in this respect between southern, eastern, and western Europe has narrowed conspicuously during the last fifteen years, and that between Japan and the West has been closed. There is a well-marked, though incomplete, trend in this direction in the temperate zone of South America: Argentina, Uruguay, and Chile. Though no significant population trend toward the regulation of births is yet apparent in Asian and North African countries (except Japan), their most eminent statesmen are now sponsoring programs designed to induce such trends.

The world regions where cultural resistance to progress in technology, education, and the purposive regulation of fertility, is likely to persist though the longest span may be tropical Latin America, tropical Africa and Indonesia—though changes will necessarily be slow throughout rural Asia. The whole developmental process may be reversed leading to chaotic situations in some countries, both in the eastern and western hemispheres.

There is a strong trend in the world today toward the purposive regulation of fertility. It can be assumed that, at least in non-Catholic populations, the purposive regulation of births will generally be achieved through contraceptive techniques. Moreover, apart from ideological resistance by Catholic forces, the only substantial resistance to the use of contraceptive techniques in achieving this goal stems from *inertia,* illiteracy, difficulties in communication, etc. Inertia is a powerful counter force, but it will eventually be overcome, except in chaotic situations, by progressive forces in the modern world.

The real question is, therefore, not "What will happen?" but "When, how, and under what conditions?"

Racial and nationalistic aspects of population policy

If this paper were being written a few years ago, it would be necessary to examine at some length the possible risks incurred in any expression of interest in the control of fertility elsewhere in the world by

American or European officials, or even by private scholars or philanthropic organizations in Western countries. The question still requires some attention, but most of its dynamite has been detonated.

There was a considerable flurry of books and articles, a quarter-century ago, about "The Rising Tide of Color," "Death of the White Peoples," "Passing of the Great Race" and so forth. The sentiments expressed in these writings were, of course, obnoxious to Asians and Africans. Presumably they have not been forgotten by some of their leaders. Moreover, this theme was played up in Communist polemics. "Neo-Malthusianism" was linked with "neo-colonialism" and "racial imperialism." It was possible to portray Western concern about the increase of population in Asia as snobbery, and to treat propaganda for its limitation as a plot to check the ascendancy of Asia and Africa in order to maintain white supremacy.

Today, one can hardly accuse Nehru of promoting birth control in India in order to support the British Raj. Nor can one plausibly argue that the Asian and African sponsors of the resolution recently passed by the Assembly of the United Nations were motivated by a desire to perpetuate white supremacy. Now the shoe is on the other foot. Asians and Africans want to act in this matter, but encounter resistance in doing so from some European governments because important elements in their population insist that the proposals advanced by these statesmen are immoral and will jeopardize the vitality and integrity of their nations.

Americans must continue to exercise restraint and to act circumspectly in dealing with this subject. Any attempt to coerce other governments as, for example, by making aid contingent on the adoption of a family limitation program (as has been rashly suggested by some enthusiasts), would obviously be resented. No responsible statesman endorses any such idea. The major question which our government now faces in this context is the extent to which it is willing to cooperate with other governments at their request in the development of projects and programs dealing with the problems of population.

The concern of some European nations about promoting their aggrandizement or security through pro-natalist policies is much less intense today than in the inter-war period, but has not entirely ceased. We will refer to this concern in another context.

Communist indifference

Again, this aspect of the questions under consideration appears in a quite different light today than it did a few years ago. This is now evident. So long as criticism of "neo-Malthusianism" served to inflame suspicion about the motives of "imperialist" and "neo-imperialist" statesmen in the minds of "oppressed" people, and to foster dissension in the non-Communist world, the Communist party played on this theme. Now that the indigenous leaders of non-European nations are engaging in programs to check mounting population growth, this theme has lost its punch and is being soft-pedalled. Moreover, in their more realistic approach to economic and social issues, the Communist governments in Eastern Europe have officially established abortion clinics and are freely promoting contraception.

The action of the Communist Bloc in abstaining from the vote on the United Nations resolution concerning population problems is perfectly logical. Communists, as such, are necessarily indifferent to all attempts to improve social conditions gradually under "capitalist" auspices. This position, however, was not taken by Yugoslavia in its statements and votes on this subject in the General Assembly.

The interest of Reformed Christianity

Many people today have forgotten that through the nineteenth and the first quarter of the twentieth century the major organs of the Anglican and Evangelical churches officially condemned contraception as immoral —though, of course, some individual clerical and lay leaders entertained different ideas. The first decisive action to the contrary was taken by the bishops of the Anglican church in the Lambeth Conference of 1930, which reversed the position taken in a similar conference ten years earlier.

Passage of the 1930 declaration of the Lambeth Conference was obviously a painful process. It reflects a concern on the part of many bishops similar to that still maintained by the leaders of the Roman church. The Anglican bishops asserted that procreation is "the primary end of marriage." They also insisted that, where there is "a clearly felt moral obligation to limit or avoid parenthood," abstinence from sexual relations is the "primary and obvious method." Nevertheless the Conference declared (193 affirmative, 67 negative) that, if there be a morally sound reason for avoiding abstinence, "other methods may be used, provided that this is done in the light of . . . Christian principles."

Some passages from a statement in 1958 by a special committee established by the Lambeth Conference of Bishops, quoted in the report of an international study group sponsored by the World Council of Churches and the International Missionary Council, reflects the change of thinking on this subject within the whole Reformed community during the last three decades:[2]

> The *means* of family planning are in large measure matters of clinical and aesthetic choice, subject to the requirement that they be admissible to the Christian conscience. . . . Christians have every right to use the gifts of science for proper ends.

[2] The quotations cited here are taken from Richard M. Fagley: *The Population Explosion and Christian Responsibility.*

The conference believes that the responsibility for deciding upon the number and frequency of children has been laid by God upon the consciences of parents everywhere: that this planning, in such ways as are mutually acceptable to husband and wife in Christian conscience, is a right and important factor in Christian family life and should be the result of a positive choice before God.

Moreover, the international study group in its report expressed the view (Paragraph 4) that "the extension of 'family planning' is one of the essential aspects of an acceptable answer to the needs of a 'world in crisis,' . . ." along with "vigorous economic and social development . . . the easing of certain pressures by means of migration, [and] the wide development of education."

Reformed Christianity no longer views contraception as inherently evil, or permissible only *in extremis,* but as a normal aspect of responsible family life. Moreover, this community now has a strong interest in the extension of family planning as contributing to the realization of sound family ideals, and as one important factor in the struggle to emancipate human beings everywhere from poverty, ignorance and disease. In this respect, Protestant Christianity joins forces with secular agencies which have similar interests.

The interests of Catholic Christianity

In view of the importance of Catholic interest in marriage and the family, we must try to understand and appreciate its position.

We can then examine the possibility of establishing a reasonable *modus vivendi* among conflicting interests in this field in a pluralistic society—in particular the United States—and in the pluralistic world order represented in the United Nations.

In origin, Catholic doctrine on sexual relations reflects the conflict that men have often experienced between intellectual and religious interests and more elemental impulses and pleasures—frequently called "the war between the spirit and the flesh." The early Christian community in the ancient world was much concerned with this issue and it influenced many theological controversies. St. Paul viewed chastity as a supreme value, though he approved of marriage. It came gradually to be assumed that the essential reason for marriage and the sexual union of spouses was the procreation of children and, as a secondary end, the "relief of concupiscence" ("It is better to marry than to burn"). St. Augustine explicitly condemned any attempt to regulate births except through abstinence. (The principal means of avoiding births in his day were *coitus interruptus* and abortion. However, he also condemned periodic avoidance of coitus at times when conception was most likely to occur, then assumed to be soon after menstruation. Some subsequent teachers took a different position on this point. It was not a major issue, prior to recent scientific discoveries concerning ovulation. Catholic tradition was, for a long time, ambivalent on this point.) The idealization of chastity is, of course, not peculiar to Catholic tradition. It has been a recurrent theme in many Christian and non-Christian religious communities. It is, as we have already noted, reflected in the statement of Anglican bishops in the 1930 Lambeth Conference.

In line with this ideal, some modern Catholic writers attribute great psychological and religious value to the practice of periodic continence. They maintain that it promotes self-discipline in all aspects of life, reinforces the mutual respect of husbands and wives, deepens their affectional life, and brings a constant sense of obedience to, and dependence on, divine guidance.[3]

The unique position of the Catholic Church as distinct from these more general ideals is grounded in the theological-metaphysical and moral doctrine of the great scholastic teacher, Thomas Aquinas, who re-worked Aristotelean philosophy in the light of Christian tradition. According to this doctrine each organic element in nature, each kind of natural action, and each divinely established institution has a final end (*finis operis*) intrinsic to its structure, as distinct from mere human intention (*finis operantis*). Catholicism seeks to bring human wills into conformity with the divine will, of which the order of nature is a partial expression. However, though intentions are taken into account, it treats the conformity of *acts* to "natural law" and to ecclesiastical law as the primary criterion of morality. Thus according to Catholic teaching, a couple may, for serious reasons, plan to avoid pregnancy though continuing to have sexual intercourse, and may try to achieve their intent by timing their sexual acts in the light of modern knowledge about the ovulatory cycle, but it is deemed immoral for them to modify the act itself to achieve this aim.

The metaphysical structure of Catholic ethics and Catholic faith in the timeless validity of its sacred tradition enforces a strong conservatism. This is illustrated in another field by the adherence through successive centuries to the doctrine, prescribed by the fifth century and more fully developed by Aquinas, that the acceptance of interest (usury) on financial loans is contrary to principles of justice and to the law of nature. A papal decree in 1830 finally gave authoritative tolerance to the acceptance of interest, within limits set by civil law, but concluded with the statement that the whole subject requires further consideration and precise formulation. According to an article in the *Dictionnaire de Droit Canonique* published in Paris in 1953, the church still maintains a reserve

---

[3] Rev. de Lestapis, is particularly eloquent on this subject. However, in the opinion of some Catholic scholars, as well as secular scientists, he makes serious errors in his attempt to present an empirical analysis of the psychological effects of contraception and related social and demographic matters. See his *Family Planning and Modern Problems: A Catholic Analysis*, 1961.

on this question. "It does not consider it useful at present to define precisely the conditions under which it is legitimate to draw income from one's money."

There have been significant developments in Catholic doctrine on marriage and procreation during the twentieth century. The definitive endorsement of periodic continence as a method of regulating births, subject only to the condition that it be for serious reasons, was an important advance. There have also been profound though subtle shifts toward increased emphasis on personal and social values in marriage. The "education" of children is firmly linked with "procreation" in defining the primary end of marriage. There are also more positive expressions of appreciation of the values of mutual respect and love in marital life. At the same time, the differentiation between the "primary" and "secondary" ends of marriage, with insistence that the latter are essentially subordinate to the former, has been reaffirmed with clarity and rigor.

There will be continuing development of Catholic doctrine in this, as in other fields. It is noteworthy that the elevation of periodic continence to a central place in Catholic teaching with respect to procreation is dependent on scientific discoveries made less than forty years ago. Pope Pius XII expressed the hope that further advances in science might fortify this principle. If a simple technique could be devised to mark some physiological process preparatory to ovulation, the "rhythm" method of regulating fertility might be widely accepted in non-Catholic as well as Catholic circles—but there is, at present, no assurance that such a technique can be devised. It is conceivable that other discoveries will offer possibilities for the development of Catholic principles that could facilitate the rational regulation of births, but it would be rash to assume that this will happen. In considering relations between Catholic and non-Catholic interests, we will proceed on the assumption that there will be no major change in Catholic *doctrine* concerning marriage and procreation within the near future. There can, however, and quite probably will be, significant changes in *emphasis* and in *political action* in this field.

The primary interest of the Catholic community in the furtherance of ethical principles firmly grounded in its tradition has at times been confused with extraneous "pro-natalist" motives. Some hostile critics have assumed that the whole structure of Catholic doctrine in this field is a scheme to increase the population of Catholic countries and the numbers of Catholics in other countries. This notion reveals a misconception of the origin and nature of Catholic doctrine, but it finds some confirmation in the writings and activities of some churchmen.

Prolific families are held in high esteem in many traditional societies. The present writer has elsewhere suggested that this is especially so in societies with unilineal kinship systems and in societies that stress military values (*Culture and Human Fertility*, UNESCO, 1954). For example, the Ashanti of central Ghana ceremonially honor a mother on the birth of her tenth child. The glory of numerous offspring is emphasized in Islamic culture, where it is associated with polygyny. There was also an idealization of prolificacy among the ancient Hebrews, a people of pastoral origin living in a fertile land surrounded by hostile nations. This ideal is reflected in many passages in the Old Testament.

This was not, however, a major theme in Western Christianity prior to the rise of modern nationalism—though in all societies there is general respect for vigorous and cohesive large families. One of the earliest expressions of national interest in the increase of population was a citation by Louis XI in the fifteenth century of a text in the Book of Proverbs: "In the multitude of people is the King's power; but in the want of people is the destruction of the prince." The first specific pro-natalist programs, offering rewards and special privileges to the fathers of large families, in modern Europe were inaugurated in the seventeenth century: (1) a Spanish Edict of 1623 and (2) a French Edict of 1666 (designed by Colbert under Louis XIV). These programs were ineffective, and pro-natalism as national policy received little further attention until the 1930's. All pronatalist programs in the German and Latin nations included attempts to suppress contraception by legal means. None of these programs, apart from the racist and political aspects of Nazi legislation, gave attention to the qualitative aspects of population trends. The Latin nations naturally sought, and received, strong support from Catholic authorities toward the achievement of their goals. Various Catholic lay organizations, in cooperation with "Large Family" leagues in various nations, gave the movement strong and active support. Activity along this line is somewhat less intense today, but it is still a real force.

The official position of the Catholic Church is still somewhat ambiguous with respect to the idealization of prolificacy without respect to conditions or motives. Catholic prelates in some countries seem to endorse indiscriminate glorification of large families. Leading Catholic ethicists, however, generally repudiate this position. They advocate rational and conscientious decisions by individual couples concerning their responsibilities in procreation. This seems to be the central position of the Catholic church, but further official clarification of this subject may be expected.

Contrary to a fairly prevalent notion, the familial attitudes and behavior of Catholics in the United States are strongly influenced by the teachings of their church—though, of course, the conformity of individuals to religious instruction on this or any other subject is usually quite imperfect. According to the Scripps-Michigan study,[4] we find that among fecund Catholic couples eighty-three per cent (as compared with ninety-three per cent of the Protestant couples) have tried in some way to regulate births. Among all Catholic couples, married ten years or more who have tried to regulate their births, sixty-two per cent had, at some

---

[4] Ronald Freedman, Pascal K. Whelpton, and Arthur A. Campbell: *Family Planning, Sterility and Population Growth in the United States,* 1959.

time, practiced periodic continence, and forty-four per cent had relied exclusively on this approved method. Thus, apparently about one-half of all fecund Catholic couples in this country, married ten years or more, have conformed to the teachings of their church, either by accepting pregnancies as they occurred without any effort to regulate fertility or by relying exclusively on the rhythm method.

Among Catholics, as among Protestants, the proportion of couples who purposively regulate their births is greater at the higher than at the lower educational levels. Moreover, among Catholics who attempt to regulate births, the proportion relying on periodic continence is positively associated with education. According to the Scripps-Michigan study, among Catholic couples who had tried in any way to regulate fertility, one-third of those with wives who had completed college, one-half of those who had completed high school, but about two-thirds of those with less schooling, resorted to contraceptive methods other than periodic continence. Effective use of rhythm (1) requires calculation of intervals, (2) is dependent to an important degree on regularity of the menstrual cycle to permit accurate records on this subject over a considerable period, and (3) requires a high degree of discipline in sexual life. These conditions seriously limit its application in populations with inferior health conditions, frequent pregnancies at short intervals and widespread illiteracy, or lack of discipline in sexual relations (as indicated by instability of marriages or high frequencies of illegitimate births).

The information reviewed above may be deemed encouraging in many respects to Catholic leaders. However, it also shows that the Catholic church faces difficult problems in this field—particularly in attempts to enforce Catholic ideals of responsible parenthood in some of the less developed countries.

The situation in Latin America, which contains one-third of all adherents to the Catholic faith, is particularly acute. Large segments of the population in this region are impoverished and illiterate. Moreover, there is great instability of conjugal unions, frequent concubinage and desertion, and illegitimate procreation in many Latin American countries. Among seventeen countries in this region for which such statistics are available, there are nine in which more than half of all births are illegitimate.

It seems reasonable to hope that the major emphasis of Catholic endeavor in Latin America in the future with respect to family relations may be directed toward promoting the legalization and stability of conjugal relations and reduction of concubinage, desertion, and "instinctual fertility," instead of placing major emphasis on the avoidance of contraception—until conditions can be established that are more conducive to adherence to the highest Catholic standards. This is, at least, a possibility to which some Catholic leaders will undoubtedly give serious consideration. Although Catholics are cautious in drawing distinctions between "greater" and "lesser" evils, they do take such distinctions into account.

The interests of the Catholic community are, of course, less *directly* involved in population trends and policies in most Asian countries, though there is strong Catholic interest in many parts of tropical Africa as well as in Latin America. The interpretation by Catholic leaders of their interests and responsibilities in this field have led them both to resist emphasis in international councils on the problematic aspects of population trends, and to resist the development of family limitation programs in any country, whether or not it is predominantly Catholic in culture.

The Catholic church can not roll back "the waves of family planning" in the modern world. It can, however, continue to apply brakes to the actions of international agencies in this field and it can delay, through indefinite periods, trends toward the purposive regulation of births in some critical areas. Continued achievement along these lines may, however, cause increasing strains in relations between governments that do and those that do not conform to Catholic policy in this respect, and within the political life of many countries.

The accommodation of religious interests in a pluralistic society

The problem with which we are concerned arises from the divergence between Catholic interests on the one hand and other religious and secular interests on the other with respect to population and parenthood. We must face this issue squarely. The Catholic church is bound by its faith to guide its communicants in accordance with the tradition that it has received. Moreover, it is bound to try to persuade all men to act in accordance with its principles. These rights and obligations of the Catholic community are entitled to respect in a pluralistic society, committed to the principle of religious toleration—just as, for example, we must respect the right and moral obligation of Quakers to protest the maintenance of our military establishment and the expenditure of public funds for armaments.

The Catholic church is not bound by its doctrine to try to compel other men to act in accordance with its teachings, or to exert *undue pressure* on political processes in an attempt to bring legislaton and other public affairs into conformity with its teachings. Any such attempt is properly resisted by those who have conflicting rights and interests. We have purposely used the elastic term "undue pressure," because there is a rather wide and undefined area between proper and improper influence on political processes in any society. Action within this area is guided by the political philosophy, judgment and conscience of the persons concerned. One related principle can, however, be stated more categorically. Though public officials must avoid unnecessary scandal or offense to any group in the nation, they must respect the rights of individuals as *per-*

sons. They can not properly try to compel persons to conform to the precepts of any church, including that to which they adhere, or refuse on this ground to serve their legitimate rights. For example, states that maintain liquor dispensaries can not properly refuse to sell liquor to Methodists.

These are basic principles of American society. Fortunately, they are clearly recognized by the most competent exponents of Catholic doctrine—though they are sometimes neglected in practice by Catholic prelates and by enthusiastic lay organizations:

> Human law is not obliged to forbid all the immoral acts from which virtuous people abstain, but only the most heinous, those from which the majority of men are able to abstain, and especially those which harm other people and the suppression of which is seen to be indispensable if a human society is to be preserved (Thomas Aquinas).
>
> The obligation of repressing moral and religious offenses cannot be an ultimate norm of action. It must be subordinated to higher and more generous norms which, in certain circumstances, allow and even perhaps make it obvious that it is better not to prevent error in order to bring about a great good. (Pope Pius XII)[5]

There has been a notable trend away from religious bigotry in the United States in recent decades. All men of good will hope that progress along this line can be carried forward. Contraception is approved and practiced by an overwhelming majority of American citizens. The proportion approving contraception must be at least as high as the proportion that approves of divorce. Both of these practices are contrary to Catholic ethics. Yet the Catholic church acquiesces in the existence of statutes in most states which permit divorce, and Catholic judges preside over divorce proceedings. The Catholic church tolerates these conditions, because in line with the principles stated by Aquinas and Pius XII, its leaders in America recognize that violent protest against the legalization of divorce would serve no useful purpose, and would engender unnecessary animosity. It is not unreasonable to assume that within the near future the Catholic church may apply the same principles with respect to official and quasi-official actions relating to the regulation of fertility. This would be a change in tactics, but it would not involve any repudiation of principles—much less a change in doctrine. Obviously, only the leaders of Catholic action in America can decide whether or not this would promote their interests. In any case, it is becoming increasingly clear that most Americans will not subject their interests in this field, as they will not with respect to divorce, to determination by Catholic teachings.

There are many indications of progress toward a *modus vivendi* in this country on this subject along the following lines: (1) firm insistence

[5] de Lestapis, *op. cit.*, p. 258.

by an increasing number of Americans on the provision of contraceptive services, by public as well as by private agencies, to individuals at their request, and on public support for research on the physiology of human reproduction, and cooperation by this nation with other nations at their request in the development of projects and programs relating to population; (2) respect by the proponents of planned parenthood for the conscientious reservations of Catholics on this subject; (3) recognition by Catholics of the sincerity of religious and secular leaders, who advocate the extension of facilities for family limitation at home and in other countries.

One indication of progress along these lines was the publication of constructive statements concerning the recent report by the National Institutes of Health on research on human reproduction, both on behalf of the National Catholic Welfare Conference and on behalf of the Planned Parenthood Federation of America—with a respectful reference in the latter to the former.

Another important statement in this field is a resolution, unanimously adopted, by the American Public Health Association. The statement was adopted by the Governing Council of the 13,000 member Association. The 162 member council includes delegates from each of the Association's 14 sections, representing the major specialities within public health, and from forty-nine affiliated state and territorial societies and regional branches. The first paragraph of the policy statement, issued by the A.P.H.A., 18 November, 1959, follows:

> There is today an increase of population which threatens the health and well-being of many millions of people. In many areas of the world substantial population increase means malnutrition and outright starvation. In other areas it may mean increased stress in fmily life, reduction of educational opportunity and the retardation of the industrial development on which a nation's rising standard of living depends. No problem—whether it be housing, education, food supply, recreation, communication, medical care—can be effectively solved today if tomorrow's population increases out of proportion to the resources available to meet those problems.

After further elaboration of the problems posed by high fertility, the resolution is concluded as follows:

> The American Public Health Association, retaining cognizance of the principle of religious freedom by all religious groups as expressed, for example, in the First Amendment of the Constitution of the United States, believes therefore that:
> 1. Public health organizations at all levels of government should give increased attention to the impact of population change on health.
> 2. Scientific research should be greatly expanded on (a) all aspects of human fertility; and (b) the interplay of biological, psychological, and socio-economic factors influencing population change.

3. Public and private programs concerned with population growth and family size should be integral parts of the health program and should include medical advice and services which are acceptable to the individuals concerned.
4. Full freedom should be extended to all population groups for the selection and use of such methods for the regulation of family size as are consistent with the creed and mores of the individuals concerned.

There will always be differences in faith, interests and ethical values among Americans. It is part of the genius of American society to welcome this diversity as a sign of freedom and vitality and, at the same time, to advance through the orderly processes established by the Constitution of the United States toward the achievement of goals endorsed by strong, though rarely unanimous, consensus. We are doing this today in the field of race relations. We will undoubtedly also do so in matters relating to population and procreation in this country and in our international relations.

Population policy in the United Nations

The Charter of the United Nations included a provision for a Population Commission subordinate to the Economic and Social Council. A unit of the Secretariat was established to carry out studies in this field and to assist the Secretary-General in the development of activities relating to population questions. Thus the importance of population in the economic and social affairs of nations is clearly recognized in the structure of the United Nations. The activities of the Commission and of the demographic unit of the Secretariat have in the past been directed to the promotion of knowledge, the exchange of ideas, the training of experts, the provision of technical assistance to member nations in the development of population studies, and the objective analysis of interrelations between population and other human affairs. The United Nations sponsored a World Population Conference in Rome in 1954, in close cooperation with the International Union for the Scientific Study of Population. This Conference was devoted wholly to "an exchange of ideas and experience" among individuals (including persons nominated by governments), invited by the Secretary-General to participate in personal capacity as "experts." No resolutions on questions of policy were considered at the Conference. The United Nations has authorized an Asian Population Conference in 1963, and a second World Population Conference in 1965.

Major issues of population policy were brought to the attention of the U.N. General Assembly in the Seventeenth Session (1962-63) by the proposal of a resolution on "Population Growth and Economic Development." The inclusion of this item in the agenda of the General Assembly necessitated the formulation of official positions on issues in this field by the governments of the various nations. The resolution was sponsored by four African nations: the United Arab Republic (which had previously taken a strong position on the importance of influencing population trends at the Conference on the Problems of Economic Development, Cairo, 1962—frequently regarded as a sequel to the Bandung Conference), Ghana, Tunisia and Uganda; four Asian nations: Ceylon, Nepal, Pakistan, and Turkey; and four European nations: Denmark, Greece, Norway and Sweden.

The introductory text includes statements that economic and social progress is dependent on education, a fair standard of living and productive work; "economic development and population growth are closely interrelated"; "the health and welfare of the family require special attention in areas with a relatively high rate of population growth"; "it is the responsibility of each government to decide its own policies and devise its own programs of action for dealing with the problems of population and economic and social progress," and recognition of the need for increased knowledge about the causes and consequences of demographic trends.

The first five operative clauses of the resolution support and provide for the expansion of the activities of the United Nations, its specialized agencies, and member governments in the investigation of population trends, their relations to economic and social development, and their implications for policy.

Article 6 of the resolution endorsed the view of the Population Commission that the United Nations should encourage and assist member governments in obtaining data and in carrying out studies on the demographic, as well as other aspects, of their development programs, and continued as follows: ". . . and that the United Nations give technical assistance, as requested by Governments, for national projects and programmes dealing with the problems of population." This item (Article 6, part 2) was the object of special attention; separate votes were taken on this item, both in Committee II (a committee of the whole where the resolution was first reviewed) and in the General Assembly.

The resolution was generally interpreted as an affirmation that population trends, especially the rapid increase of population in the less developed countries, present serious problems which the various governments should study with a view to forming appropriate policies and operational programs. It was assumed in the discussion that in many countries these programs would include the provision of facilities for family limitation, though the sponsors of the resolution insisted that some governments might with good reason adopt radically different policies. Although explicit authorization for technical assistance by the United Nations to governments at their request in the development of operative programs in this field was limited to Article 6, part 2, it was generally recognized that the resolution as a whole tended to remove restraints on the freedom of action by agencies of the United Nations in extending cooperation to governments at their request in the development of programs designed to affect population trends and related aspects of health and welfare—at least in preliminary investigations relevant to the formation of policies and programs in this field. A statement by a representative of the government of the United States (quoted below) tended to confirm this implication. It is, therefore, not surprising that some governments opposed the whole resolution, questioned the competence of the General Assembly to act on the resolution, and urged that it be withdrawn by its sponsors. Such opposition was, for example, presented with vigor by the Argentinian and Irish delegations. This opposition helped to clarify the significance of the proposal and of its final adoption, albeit without the most controversial item (Article 6, part 2).

The alignment today of the governments represented in the United Nations on these issues is reflected in their votes on the second part of Article 6 in the General Assembly (after the clarification of issues by the discussion in Committee II, and opportunity for consultations between delegations and their governments). There were thirty-four votes in the Assembly in favor of this item, thirty-four votes in opposition, and thirty-two abstentions.

The position of the United States Delegation in abstaining on this point, as stated to the General Assembly by Richard N. Gardner, was as follows:

> In the opinion of the United States, operative paragraph 6 does not add or subtract from the authority which the United Nations already possesses as a result of resolutions of the General Assembly and of the Economic and Social Council concerning the granting of technical assistance upon request to member nations. In our view this paragraph is superfluous.
>
> While the United States believes that the authority to lend technical assistance in all aspects of population problems already exists, we also believe . . . that assistance by the United Nations should emphasize those three areas in which there appears to be broad agreement among member governments, namely, the encouraging and assisting of member governments to obtain factual *information* on the demographic aspects of their economic and social development; the *training* of nationals of members for demographic work; and the promotion of full and responsible *discussion* of population problems." (Quoted, with italics, from *The Department of State Bulletin,* Jan. 7, 1963) .

In discussing the situation, Mr. Gardner gave an exposition of the general position of the government of the United States on the international aspects of population problems. This nation is concerned about the social consequences of population trends both here and elsewhere in the world; it recognizes that in the less developed countries present levels of population growth may constitute a major obstacle to the realization of developmental goals. It will not suggest policies or programs in the field to any other government, and it insists that no obstacles be placed in the way of governments which, in the light of their own needs and values, seek solutions to their population problems. It recognizes the great need for more knowledge on this subject, including "more facts about alternative methods of family planning." This nation will help other countries at their request "to find potential sources of information and assistance on ways and means of dealing with population problems."

The discussion and votes mainly reflected concern about the effect of population trends on economic and social development, on the one hand, and opposition to family limitation on ideological grounds on the other—though, of course, the opponents also questioned the validity of the economic arguments advanced by proponents of the resolution. The voting was, nevertheless, undoubtedly influenced in some cases by political alignments on other issues. Also, some of the proponents revealed in the discussion that they were more concerned about maintaining the rights of nations and individuals to manage their own affairs than about the economic effects of population trends in their own countries.

During the preliminary review in Committee II, action was taken on various proposed revisions. The motion to strike out Article 6, Part 2, was rejected at that time by a narrow margin. The resolution as a whole (*including* this controversial item on which the United States had abstained) was then approved by forty-three affirmative votes (including that of the United States), with fourteen votes in opposition, and forty-four abstentions. The fourteen states which cast negative votes at this time were: Argentina, Austria, Belgium, Colombia, France, Ireland, Italy, Lebanon, Liberia, Luxembourg, Peru, Portugal, Spain, Uruguay. The nations which abstained at this time from action on the motion as a whole included the Communist bloc, seven African countries of French expression, also Ethiopia, Sierra Leone, Sudan, and Tanganyika, eight Latin American or Caribbean countries, the Philippines, Canada, and the Netherlands. In the General Assembly the resolution as a whole (without Article 6, part 2) was approved by sixty-nine affirmative votes, with no votes in opposition, and twenty-seven abstentions.

The action on this resolution obviously marks the beginning, rather than the conclusion, of the active consideration of issues relating to national population policies in the United Nations.

CONSIDERATIONS ON AMERICAN POPULATION TRENDS

Trend of total population

Contemporary American culture induces a level of fertility well above that sufficient for the replacement of the parental generations. This cultural force has three essential components: (1) strong preference for married life, (2) strong interest in children and aversion to childless or one-child families, and (3) diversity among individuals in parental goals along with a clustering of preferences by a large majority of couples within the range of two to four children.

Data (as yet unpublished) from the 1960 Scripps-Michigan study show that among white wives aged thirty years or more, or married more than ten years, about nine per cent of the children born to them are admittedly in excess of the numbers they had wanted. This is a minimum figure. It is limited to white couples. It does not include the results of unwanted pregnancies, still in progress, or illegitimate births to women who were still unmarried or were divorced at the time of the study. If these limitations could be taken into account and adjustments made for age distribution and parity, the figure might be raised to around fifteen per cent. It is also possible that on more severe criteria, the proportions of "unwanted" births (with respect to size of family apart from errors in timing) might be considerably higher. It is possible that in some cases women who did not really want another pregnancy may reinterpret their preferences after its occurrence. Moreover, there is undoubtedly a marginal, indecisive area in preferences concerning procreation. If the addition of another child required a positive decision rather than merely permissive acceptance of the consequences of sexual union, families might be smaller than indicated at present by explicit statements about excess fertility. However, the statements of recently married husbands and wives concerning their intentions show that even under these conditions the wanted sizes of family would not be far below those now being attained. They would quite certainly remain above the replacement level. Moreover, the proportion of wanted births that is lost due to sterility or impairments of fecundity is very considerable—larger than the ratio of excess births to the number apparently wanted. Further progress in the correction of impairments to fecundity may, therefore, more or less offset continued progress toward universality and efficacy in the regulation of fertility.

Apart from the effects of a catastrophe such as war or a prolonged depression, any radical change in the reproductive trend of the American population can only result from rather profound changes in present cultural values—such as a rising aversion to marriage or parenthood, greater indifference to the regulation of births, or a marked increase in preferences for large families. A return to somewhat later ages at marriage might bring an appreciable, though hardly a drastic, reduction in levels of fertility. None of these possible changes seem imminent at present, though changes in values and ways of living during the coming decades may influence future population trends in ways that can not now be foreseen.

There is no consensus among economists concerning the optimum rate of change in the population of the United States, and there are widely divergent views on this subject. This indicates the complexity of the economic consequences of alternative possibilities within the range of reasonable expectations. It may also indicate that economic analysis on this subject is incomplete and requires more intensive investigation. In view of the degree to which the present trend of population in this country is determined by the personal interests of our citizens, it could scarcely be affected by any generally acceptable measures intended to influence reproduction directly—except measures to increase still further the availability and efficacy of methods for the regulation of births.

In view of the probable continuation of rather rapid increase of population in America, it is important that increased attention be directed to the conservation of natural resources. (See Chapters 5 and 6.) It is much simpler to establish the national interest in certain lands and other resources before they are intensively used for commercial and other private ends than after this has happened. Moreover, many scientists have recently insisted that serious and far-reaching consequences affecting the natural basis of life sometimes result in quite unforeseen ways from acts intended only to serve limited and specific ends.

Apart from the need for more intensive study of the implications of population increase in America and the importance of appropriate conservation policies, the most reasonable over-all national policy on the basis of our present knowledge with respect to the trend of our national population is, perhaps, a policy of *laissez-faire*—specifically in the sense of accepting and respecting the interests and preferences of individuals in questions relating to procreation.

Regional and racial trends

Dr. Bogue in Chapter 5 has summarized regional and racial trends which pose important policy issues.

Differences in reproductive trends among racial elements of the American population are due mainly to differences in the regional location and in the distribution of these elements by economic and social levels, though they may also be influenced to some extent by differences in cultural traditions. Although the proportion now living in cities is slightly higher among Negroes than among whites, many Negroes now living in cities are recent migrants who carry over patterns of behavior and attitudes acquired in a rural setting. According to 1950 census data, social class differences in fertility were greater among nonwhites than among whites. At given social levels Negroes and whites generally have similar levels of fertility. But among Negroes the high proportion of persons of meager education, limited occupational skills, and low income —among whom contraception is less widely and less effectively practiced than in the middle and upper educational levels—raises the reproductivity of this segment well above the general average.

These considerations suggest that the analysis of demographic trends and the treatment of population problems can, at least in large part, be carried out effectively, without reference to race, wholly in terms of geographical, social and personal characteristics. This approach will be increasingly appropriate as diverse racial elements in our population become more effectively integrated in all aspects of American life, and as differences in racial origin, already attenuated and confused by interracial unions (mainly illegal and exploitative in the past), become increasingly blurred. This process is being accelerated by the entry of persons from Puerto Rico, Hawaii, and South America where racial lines are already crossed. We will generally focus attention here on the treatment of population questions in functional terms which are more objective and less ambiguous. Yet in spite of these limitations, classification by race or color is still useful in treatment of many issues, because the behavior of persons with distinct cultural background is affected both by their own traditions and experience and by the attitudes of other persons toward them.

The migratory movements noted in the preceding paragraphs have relieved the situation of people in areas of relatively low opportunity. The outmovement of people and inmovements of investment and economic enterprises have fostered, in some measure, a trend toward equalization of opportunity between the situations from which the migrants have come and those to which they have moved. And the continuation of these movements is evidence that the migrants have in general improved their positions. At the same time, the influx of large elements with relatively limited education and industrial skills have aggravated civic problems in metropolitan areas which have received them. The beneficial effects of these movements might have been achieved with less strain, and with less problematic effects if (1) the initial disparities in education, income, etc. had been less extreme and (2) the natural increase of persons in situations of limited opportunity were reduced to the level prevailing in the rest of the nation.

The movements of people and enterprises into metropolitan areas—great congregations of industry, commerce, and persons, spreading out through politically disjointed areas, creates some of the most acute problems of contemporary American society. One aspect of this development is a trend toward economic and social, as well as racial, segregation in the component units of these aggregations, with greater resources and superior schools for the children of parents with relatively high income and educational experience, but inferior opportunities for the children of parents with less income and schooling, many of whom have been drawn from relatively backward areas.

Urbanism as the pervasive mode of life of a great nation is a relatively new phenomenon in human experience—at least since the time of city civilizations of the ancient Mediterranean world. Many of the problems which it poses, though created or at least intensified by population trends, lie outside the scope of population policy as usually conceived. The trend itself can not be reversed. It must, therefore, be met by appropriate adaptations in political, economic and social institutions. We limit ourselves at this point to noting one general, obvious implication. The nation is an interacting demographic unit. The processes of personality formation and the acquisition of skills by people in Vermont, Puerto Rico, the Carolinas and the Dakotas are matters of vital importance to the citizens of New York, Detroit and Los Angeles. The population elements entering their civic life are in large part formed in other localities, some of which may be geographically distant. This points up the importance of actions designed to promote comparable levels of health, education and opportunity throughout the nation, while preserving so far as possible the positive values of diverse traditions, varied personal interests, and individual initiative.

Immigration

Slightly over 270,000 immigrants were admitted to the United States in 1961 (a fairly representative year); their admission added 1.5 per 1,000 persons in our population. Through the last decade, the increment by net immigration has equaled about one-tenth of that resulting from the excess of births over deaths. Thus immigration now is a minor though not a negligible factor in the increase of the nation.

No responsible leader in this country advocates, and no responsible statesman elsewhere expects, a return to the era of unrestricted international migration. On the other hand, it is generally thought that immigration in moderate volume benefits the United States and it is clearly recognized that a drastic curtailment of immigration would engender intense resentment in many countries, as well as in large segments of our own population. As the richest country in the world, aspiring to play a major role in international affairs, we are especially vulnerable to envy and suspicion. Our wealth is, of course, due in part to the circumstance that a relatively small population, recruited mainly through immigration, now occupies the temperate zone of a vast continent rich in natural resources. We are also indebted to the heritage of Western civilization, to the stimulus of diverse cultural traditions, and perhaps to self-selective factors in the migration process. It would jeopardize our security to lock our doors at this point against any further entries to this land of opportunity. *Richesse oblige*—as does *noblesse*. Moreover, there is a widespread belief that such action would tend to stultify our culture.

Assuming that immigration will normally be limited to some fixed amount—or, more reasonably, some fixed proportion of our population at different times—there is no clear basis for determining a precisely appropriate ratio. Many would advocate a higher ratio than that now in effect, i.e., 1.5 per 1,000 population. Others would insist on maintaining this or an even lower figure. Any decision on this question will presumably represent a compromise between conflicting preferences.

The distribution of opportunities for the entrance of aliens to this country is a more complex, and a rather more critical question. The ingenious quota principle which was in many respects appropriate to conditions in the 1920's is far less relevant to conditions in the world today. Of the 271,000 aliens admitted as immigrants in 1961, only 96,000 entered by quota. Moreover, 22,000 of these were in preferential categories— either as persons admitted because of special skills or abilities (7,000, including members of their families) or as the near kin of persons already present (15,000). "Preferred" immigrants could have been admitted with equal or greater convenience if there were no quota system. This leaves only 74,000 aliens otherwise admitted through operation of the quota system—i.e., 27 per cent of all immigrants. Nearly 33,000 wives, husbands, or children of American citizens were admitted without reference to quotas. These admissions *plus* the preferred classes mentioned above accounted for 56,000 entries in 1961—over twenty per cent of the total.

Immigrants originating in the Western Hemisphere, to which the quota system does not apply, numbered 113,000—over forty per cent of the total. Using the classification of all immigrants in the same year by country of birth, the principal sources of inter-American immigration to this country (excluding, of course, entries from Puerto Rico and the Virgin Islands) are, in order of importance:

Mexico:	42,000
Canada, Newfoundland, etc.:	33,000
West Indies:	22,000
South America:	15,000
Central America:	7,000

The total of these figures, 119,000, is larger than the number admitted on the basis of origin in this hemisphere, 113,000, because the former includes some persons entering under other categories. The large figure for Mexicans does not include the nearly 300,000 persons who entered legally as temporary agricultural workers, because these workers do not acquire permanent status as alien residents. Incidentally, the problem of the illegal entry of Mexican workers has been largely solved—or, at least, greatly reduced. Outside the classes listed above there were 30,000 immigrants (eleven per cent of the total). They include persons admitted under special laws applicable to refugees and unassimilated elements in certain countries (Greece, Italy, Netherlands, Portugal), plus minor adjustment categories.

The quota system is limited in its operation by the allotment of more than half of its hypothetical total to two countries, Great Britain and Ireland, whereas more than half of these options are never used.

Prospective immigrants from other European countries resent these vacant allotments. Prospective migrants from Asia view the nominal quotas allocated to their countries as an expression of racist intolerance in America—although our nation now includes one prosperous state in which a majority of citizens are Asian in origin. On the other hand, the rapid growth of population and lagging productivity in Central and South America (which altogether have a population nearly a hundred times that of Puerto Rico) stimulate an emergent impetus toward opportunities in North America. The United States may soon find it very difficult either to absorb the potential influx from Latin America or to arrest it without unfortunate political consequences. Certainly any attempt at this time to assign quotas to various American countries would be bitterly resented.

An objective review of present and emergent trends suggests that, however useful it may have been at one time, the quota system of regulating immigration to the United States is now an obsolete and embarrassing apparatus.

The logical alternative would seem to be some universally applicable system of accepting immigrants, within a specified total, as individuals without reference to race or national origin. Such a system could include a combination of three principles: (1) the exclusion of persons who do not meet established standards of literacy, health, etc.; (2) expansion of the principles of preferential admission already in force with respect to (a) special skills or abilities and (b) kinship to citizens or aliens already present in this country, in line with the original aim of the quota system, but free from its arbitrary and invidious aspects; (3) chance or priority of application, or some other methods of random selection among other applicants without respect to race or country of origin. The basic program might be supplemented, if need be, by *ad hoc* measures to meet emergency situations. There might also, if this is deemed wise, be some special provision for the admission of immigrants from the two countries bordering the United States to the north and south, i.e., Canada and Mexico.

In view of changing demographic, economic and political conditions and the responsibility of the United States in world affairs, there is urgent need for serious reconsideration of all aspects of American immigration policy.

Problematic aspects of employment, culture and reproduction

Inadequate opportunity for employment, which is essential to decent living and self-respect, is a cancer in American society. The inability of many young persons to find their places in the national economy is especially demoralizing at a critical point in their lives. It is a major factor in the prevalence of juvenile delinquency. Yet three to five million persons of all ages, i.e., four to seven per cent of the labor force, have been out of work in this country at any given time during the last ten years. The average proportion of the labor force out of work in 1961 was six and seven tenths per cent; among would-be workers fifteen to nineteen years the figure is fifteen per cent, and among those twenty to twenty-four years ten per cent. The problem of unemployed youth has special urgency at this time due to an expected rise from 1960 to 1970 of forty-five per cent in the number of potential young workers, fifteen to twenty-four years old. (See Chapter 5.) The problem also has chronic aspects that are rooted in the structure of our society.

The level of employment is obviously in part a cyclical phenomenon, rising in periods of economic expansion and declining in recessions. Unemployment is, also, in part, a local problem, caused by shifts in the location of enterprises and in the employment demands of particular industries (e.g., mining), which leave stranded workers who can not move or adjust to new opportunities without friction, delay and loss. These problems involve critical economic issues outside the scope of the present discussion.

Technological advance in general, and automation in particular, eliminate some employment needs and creates others. As an answer to these needs, we place major reliance on formal education. Commercial and industrial enterprises, in turn prescribe achievement in school as a condition of entry to many types of employment. But the expansion of education is imperfect, leaving gaps and lags. Moreover, the school can only function within the community. Its activities are conditioned by forces outside its control. It is only one among many agencies that affect the formation of children's interests, drives and personality. It is probably less powerful in this respect than the homes in which children are reared and their informal associations with companions. These, in turn, are influenced by mass media which, in this country, are controlled mainly by commercial interests. Finally, the maintenance of standards is an essential aspect of the educational process. Many children, handicapped by limitations in their home environment, beset by usual burdens, distractions or emotional problems, or deficient in genetic endowment experience repeated frustration in the classroom. In many cases their special needs could be met, and sometimes they are met, by extraordinary effort and especially skillful instruction. But teachers, too, are human and communities usually provide only limited support. So the available resources for meeting their needs are often inadequate. Accordingly many youngsters coming to maturity in the United States today have a marginal, precarious position in the economic and social life of the nation.

The military establishment rejects about one-eighth of the nation's youth as incapable of absorbing the required military training within a reasonable length of time—or, in other words, as *militarily unemployable*. This figure excludes rejections solely for medical reasons or because of physical disabilities, or on other grounds such as criminal records. The men rejected on mental grounds are those who have not received or have not absorbed sufficient schooling to enable them to acquire, without undue cost to the establishment, the skills required for military activity. This takes account of the need for servicemen today to handle rather complex equipment, and the necessity of assigning many men to the technical, clerical, and organizational aspects of military affairs.

The proportions who do not qualify mentally for military service are higher among draftees than among volunteers. Within the whole military manpower pool, including volunteers for all branches of the service, thirteen per cent were rejected on mental grounds, from August 1950 through July 1960 (including those who also had physical disabilities).[6] In 1961, twenty-three per cent of all drafted men were rejected because of poor performance on mental tests.

Youths who "drop out" from school as soon as this is legally permissible tend to become *marginal workers* in the civilian economy. These are largely youths who experienced a sense of frustration in the school situation. According to the results of a survey described by the Bureau of Labor Statistics, it was found that among those who left school in 1961 and did not attend college and had entered the labor market, twenty-seven per cent of the dropouts, as compared with eighteen per cent of the graduates, were unemployed in October of that year. Among youths then in the labor market who left school the previous year, seventeen per cent of the dropouts as compared with twelve per cent of the graduates were unemployed; in the case of those who left school two years earlier the proportion was still seventeen per cent for the dropout but only eight per cent for the graduates; finally, in the case of those under twenty-four years who had been out of school three years or more, the proportions were thirteen per cent and seven per cent, respectively. (*Special Labor Force Report*, No. 21, May, 1962, Table 4.) The unemployment rates were similar for males and females.

Men rejected for military service may feel a sense of relief. They can apply for jobs, drive around if they or friends get a car, marry and start their families. But many of them must also have a sense of chagrin. Those who drop out of school may also enjoy their freedom; but they, too, may reproach themselves or society. Those who seek work but are denied a place, or who are taken on and soon laid off, feel no relief but only disappointment or bitterness. Rejectees, dropouts, and marginal workers become, in James Conant's phrase, "social dynamite."

If these facts are treated seriously they suggest three possible implications for national policy.

(1) The first suggestion is perhaps the most radical but it has the merit that it could be applied immediately to the situation that already exists. This is the inauguration of large public enterprises capable of

---

[6] Karpinos, Bernard D., *Qualifications of American Youth for Military Service*, Department of the Army, Table 5.

absorbing all marginal workers in activities that are not profitable as commercial undertakings but which would benefit the nation—though not necessarily in goods or services equal in value to their cost. This would require a large investment in the social health of the nation, without comparable material or military value. This may be a shocking notion. A large increase in police forces may seem more acceptable to many citizens, because it is less dependent on an imaginative comprehension of insidious trends.

(2) A second suggestion is more conventional and is supported by strong organizations. It is also a matter of vital importance. There is need for enlarged investment in the quality of educational services throughout the nation, especially at the elementary and high school levels—including provision for smaller classes and special programs adapted to the needs of children with different abilities, as well as improvements in facilities. This can not help those who have left or are leaving school, but it can improve the prospects of those now enrolled or entering school—and of their children.

(3) A third possibility rests on the hypothesis that many of those rejected for military service, those who drop out of school, and those who become marginal workers come from homes in which there are more children than their parents want to support, including the children of unmarried women. This proposition can not be conclusively demonstrated, but it is very reasonable. In that case, facilitation of the control of fertility—especially among persons at low educational levels where such control is now least prevalent and least effective—might appreciably lessen the problem under consideration in later years. This is a long-range proposition with respect to its effect on the next generation; but it could also bring some immediate relief to families now in straightened circumstances. Action along this line merits serious consideration, along with other measures such as those suggested above. It has the advantage of requiring relatively small expenditure of public funds.

According to the Scripps-Michigan study mentioned above, among apparently fecund white couples in the United States in 1955, with wives aged fifteen to thirty-nine years classified by education, over ninety per cent of those with college or high school education had practiced some method of regulating pregnancies, but only seventy-eight per cent of those who had not progressed beyond the elementary grades had done so. Furthermore, among fecund white couples who had tried to control their fertility, the proportions who had given birth to more children than they wanted run as follows: among those with college experience, eight per cent; high school, four years, eleven per cent; high school, one to three years, sixteen per cent; grade school only, thirty-two per cent. Among non-white couples with only elementary schooling, the proportions who have not practiced any method of regulating births and who, even if they have tried, have not done so effectively is presumably at least

as high as among white couples with equally limited education. Among
ever-married women aged forty to forty-four years in the United States in
1950, the number of children ever born per white woman was 2.33 as a
general average, but 3.26 per white women with less than eight years of
schooling. The comparable figure per nonwhite ever-married women with
less than eight years schooling was slightly lower: 3.05—due to the higher
frequency of childlessness (due largely to sterility) among nonwhites
(twenty-six per cent), as compared with whites, (fourteen per cent) at this
educational level. The children of parents with inferior education who
have larger families than they want, or can properly support, begin life
with severe handicaps. Then too, more than five per cent of all registered
births in the United States—2.2 per cent of the white births and 21.8 per
cent of the nonwhite births—are illegitimate (1959 dates, adjusted in the
National Office of Vital Statistics for states not reporting births by
legitimacy at that time, but not adjusted for possible omissions or mis-
reporting). Many of these children enter life with handicaps.

It has been proposed by some persons that any women who bears
two illegitimate children should be sterilized by court order. This savors
of "cruel and unusual punishment," and a law to this effect might be
declared unconstitutional. In any case, it is repugnant to American ideals.

On the other hand, assistance by public agencies to couples who
wish to avoid having additional children and who request such assistance,
either through the provision of contraceptive services or by sterilization of
husband or wife, at the discretion of those immediately concerned, would
be wholly consistent with individual rights—assuming that no attempt is
made to influence persons to act contrary to their own will and conscience. Such action might also be deemed conducive to the public interest.

The relatively high frequency of illegitimate births in this country,
which seems to have been rising during the last decade, presents even
more difficult problems. There is a strong argument for more strenuous
endorsement of the requirement that the fathers of illegitimate children
provide for their support; but in practice this is so difficult that no great
change can be expected as the result of efforts along this line. Many
women who have borne one or more children out of wedlock may later
marry and want to bear children to their husbands. Therefore, sterilization is not a procedure likely to be requested by most unmarried mothers
or generally recommended to them by conscientious physicians. These
considerations do not apply to the provision of contraceptive services in
such circumstances. However, very improvident persons, even though
they may view an additional pregnancy as a calamity, may be negligent in
contraceptive practice. Some persons have proposed that abortion be
made available to unmarried women on certification by a social agency
that neither the woman nor her family is able to make proper provision
for the nurture of the child. The medical risk of abortion by a competent

physician within three months of conception does not exceed the risk of allowing normal completion of the pregnancy and, unlike proposals for compulsory sterilization, this would not violate the rights of the woman concerned. However, authorization of such action would require legislation to which there are grave objections. The birth each year of 200,000 illegitimate babies brings a trail of misfortunes, but there are no simple, effective and generally acceptable ways of overcoming this evil.

We have proceeded in the foregoing discussion on the hypothesis that individual differences in intelligence and personality are mainly determined by environmental forces. This is a popular assumption, but there is much scientific evidence to the contrary from studies of twins, adopted children, degrees of kinship, etc. Genetic and environmental factors interact in such intricate ways that their relative roles cannot be measured precisely, but variations in genetic endowment are surely important. However, for present purposes, this question is largely academic. If the operation of genetic and environment factors in determining the characteristics of individual Americans could be assessed precisely, it is difficult to see how this would lead to any different implications with respect to national policies from those to which we have already given consideration—except that a clear indication of the importance of heredity would give added impetus to some measures that are socially desirable for other reasons. Knowledge about human genetics does have immediate relevance to certain problems affecting particular families, but these do not, for the most part, involve large demographic issues.

In dealing with problems of unemployment, culture, and reproduction, we have focused attention on younger segments of the population. Unemployment is also acute at the other end of the age scale, among aged persons. This problem has been aggravated by increase in the proportion of aged persons in the total population during the first half of the twentieth century. There will be only a moderate increase in this proportion from 1960 to 2000—though a jump can then be expected as the wave of new recruits now entering the labor market reaches advanced ages.

The problem of poverty in old age is a serious one, but it is not mainly a demographic issue. One aspect of this question that should, however, be considered from this angle concerns the distribution of aged persons by region and type of community. The proportion of persons over sixty-five years of age was higher in 1960 in the non-metropolitan population (9.9 per cent) than in the metropolitan population (8.5 per cent). The proportion was, however, somewhat higher in the non-farm than in the farm segment of the non-metropolitan population. Aged persons cannot respond to changes in the distribution of economic opportunities as can younger persons. Many aged persons, especially among those with assured income, do move to areas where living is less expensive or more attractive. But many others must pass the remainder of their days in areas of declining opportunity, and they often encounter real hardship. Their situation demands special attention.

We have noted certain currents within the nation's population, and have considered some ways in which possible modifications of these trends might be socially advantageous. We may have neglected some important issues and the situations that we have examined presumably have implications that we have overlooked. We return, in concluding this chapter, to a major principle advanced in considering the trend of our population as a whole. We assume that any measure in the realm of national population policy must be consistent with the rights and interests of individuals. This principle, we believe, is a basic premise of American democracy.

Final Report of the Twenty-third American Assembly

At the close of their discussions the participants in the Twenty-third American Assembly at Arden House, Harriman, New York, May 2-5, 1963, on *The Population Dilemma,* reviewed as a group the following statement. Although there was general agreement on the final report, it is not the practice of The American Assembly for participants to affix their signatures, and it should not be assumed that every participant necessarily subscribes to every recommendation.

Never before in history have the security and welfare of mankind been so indivisible. Never before has man acquired the capability of achieving his own extinction. These circumstances require him to marshal his intelligence, control his emotions, and rise above his traditional thought and action in an unprecedented way. Failure to do so may threaten not only his prosperity, security and peace, but also his survival.

Among the serious threats to welfare and security, and therefore to peace, is the accelerating rate of world population growth. The less tangible but very real injury to personal development and the maintenance of family life must also be of concern. Rapid population increase and its accompaniments are obstructing economic development, and thereby contributing to frustration, social unrest and political instability in many areas of the globe. Rapid population growth also contributes to complex problems in the United States.

The Twenty-third American Assembly believes that:

A. Present and prospective world rates of population growth cannot be maintained indefinitely. Such growth contributes substantially to the perpetuation of low levels of living for two-thirds of mankind, and creates difficult problems of adjustment in the economically advanced nations.

B. World birth rates must be reduced in view of the reductions in death rates already achieved.

C. Reduction of family size would produce important gains for many families as well as for entire nations. Unrestricted fertility tends to damage the health of the mother, impairs family life and restricts opportunity for adequately rearing and educating children.

The time has come for vigorous and coordinated action to alert mankind to the need for a reduced rate of population growth and to develop multilateral and bilateral programs to assist nations which desire to reduce their fertility.

I. World Problems

A high birth rate obstructs the economic development of low income countries in a number of ways. It diverts resources and hampers economic growth in the less developed economies and makes it necessary to provide for a larger population rather than for a higher level of living. It contributes to imbalance in rural-urban and regional population distribution. It generates an age structure with large numbers of young dependents in relation to workers. It impairs efforts to improve the quality of a population by restricting per capita expenditures for improving health, raising educational levels, and teaching new occupational skills. It reduces natural resources per capita.

Reducing the birth rate and thereby lowering the rate of population increase is of course not the complete solution to the improvement of economic conditions in the less developed areas. It is a major element; but other factors—social and economic—are also involved. These include capital investment, technology, diversification of the economy, distribution of income, occupational skills, entrepreneurship, and attitudes and institutions favorable to innovation and social reform. The expansion of international trade and investment would also contribute to economic advance. More effective utilization of natural resources is required; in the short run world resources are sufficient to permit rising levels of living.

International migration can help many persons and temporarily ease some population pressures. It cannot, however, solve the world's major population problems.

Recommendations

The United Nations and the Specialized Agencies should:

1. *Expand activities in the field of population.*

They have significantly improved population data and research. They should now undertake more comprehensive and intensive population research, particularly on the interrelationships of population, economics and social change, and develop more effective programs for the dissemination of its findings.

2. *Expand and strengthen the population staff and the regional population training and research centers.*

This would enable the agencies better to assist nations to comprehend their own problems and formulate appropriate solutions.

3. *Provide direct aid to countries wishing assistance in family planning programs.*

The World Health Organization and other international agencies should recognize the consequences of their great achievements in reducing death rates; they should assist nations in dealing with the resultant population growth.

4. *Encourage and support, especially through the WHO, biological and medical research in human reproduction.*

5. *Strive to contribute to the growing world consciousness of the implications of population growth through appropriate revisions of and additions to youth and adult educational materials prepared for world distribution by UNESCO.*

II. THE POSITION OF THE UNITED STATES ON WORLD POPULATION PROBLEMS

The "Statement of United States Policy" to the 17th General Assembly of the United Nations represents an important step forward. It offers the assistance of the United States to nations, upon request, "to find potential sources of information and assistance on ways and means of dealing with population problems." This policy should explicitly recognize that:

(1) Population growth in all countries affects the destinies of the world's people. It is an international problem of concern to all. (2) Parents everywhere should be free to decide how many children they should have. (3) Sustained progress in economic well-being requires the reduction of population increase.

Recommendations

In view of the relation of population to economic and social development, and the need for bilateral as well as multilateral programs of technical assistance, it is recommended that:

1. *Since the ultimate objective of foreign aid is to improve living conditions, the United States give consideration to the way in which developmental plans are affected by population trends.*

2. *The United States extend assistance to developing nations, at their request, for the investigation of population problems and in support of programs to promote the voluntary regulation of fertility.*

3. *Administrative means be established by the federal government for disseminating knowledge about population problems and methods of regulating family size.*

Such action is needed to implement the statement by President Kennedy of April 24, 1963, that the government could support increased research in fertility and human reproduction, and make the results more available to the world so that everyone could make his own judgment.

III. DOMESTIC POPULATION POLICY

There must be a greater concern by our national, state and local governments with our own population problems.

The postwar resurgence in population growth coupled with the growth of metropolitan areas has created complex problems not only at the state and local levels but also on a regional and national basis.

Rapid population growth has undoubtedly contributed to additional effective demand and thus to increased economic growth. Although there are no insuperable economic difficulties in the short run, we see increasing dangers in the continuation of the present rate of growth that would double the population every forty years with the prospect of constricted social opportunities and progressive crowding.

Accelerated population growth has already intensified problems of urban congestion, education and transportation, and contributed to pollution of air and water and crowding of outdoor recreational facilities. It has required federal, state and local governments to provide new and expanded public facilities and services, with consequent increased taxation. Furthermore, the wave of young workers now entering the labor force constitutes a serious challenge to our economy, which is already confronted by readjustment to the advent of automation. These challenges will require special attention.

Recommendations

This American Assembly therefore recommends:

1. *Intensified investigation of our population trends and problems—including their long-range as well as their short-term implications.*

2. *Accelerated research through the United States Public Health Service and private agencies, on the biological and medical aspects of human reproduction so that a variety of improved methods of fertility control are developed.*

3. *Assumption of responsibility by the federal, state and local governments for making available information concerning the regulation of fertility and providing services to needy mothers compatible with the religious and ethical beliefs of the individual recipient.*

Freedom of decision regarding family size is a basic human right which in practice is now effectively withheld from a portion of the American people. This discrimination would be eliminated by making fully available to all adults through public and private agencies information and service regarding the various methods of family planning which accord with the ethical and religious convictions of those involved.

4. *The cultivation with the assistance of schools, religious organizations and other cultural media, of a sense of responsibility concerning marriage and parenthood, including the responsibility of bringing into the world only those children whom parents are prepared adequately to care for and educate.*

5. *Recognition that the United States is an economic and social unit, to the end that all of our citizens, no matter what their area of origin or race, are adequately prepared for full participation in the life of any part of the nation.*

Since the end of the war, millions of persons have moved to urban parts of the United States. Many are ill-prepared for life in the areas to which they moved. In consequence, problems of accommodation are severe for the migrants and for the communities to which they come.

6. *Our immigration policy should be in accord with the following principles:*

a. selection among applicants without discrimination by race or country or origin
b. total immigration not to exceed the present level except in emergencies
c. exclusion of persons who do not meet established personal standards such as those relating to literacy and health, save under extraordinary circumstances
d. consideration of 1) special skills, abilities and employment opportunities, and 2) kinship to persons already present in this country

7. *The acceleration of economic growth and increased employment opportunities in view of the current levels of unemployment and the impending increase in the labor force.*

8. *More research on the resources of the United States and*

*other parts of the world with attention to the lessening of waste
and protection of the claims of oncoming generations.*[1]

9. *Appointment by the President of the United States of a
Commission to inform, after investigation, the government and the
American people of the nature of population problems at home and
abroad with respect to: implications for all aspects of American life,
and relevance to our efforts, in cooperation with international agencies, to promote economic and social progress throughout the world.*

* * *

The vast majority of the people of the world, including a large
proportion of the people of the United States, do not yet recognize the
full implications of present population trends. The Twenty-third American Assembly cannot emphasize too strongly that time is running out
for the formulation and implementation of world and national population policy.

To continue to ignore world and United States population problems
is to ignore the welfare and security of all peoples. We must not remain
complacent in the face of a major threat to world peace and survival.

Participants in the Twenty-third
American Assembly

AKERS, MILBURN P.
Editor
Chicago *Sun-Times*
Illinois

ALEXANDER, E. RUSSELL, M.D.
University of Washington
School of Medicine
Seattle

AUSTIN, LEWIS C.
Harriman Scholar
Columbia University

BARNETT, ROBERT W.
Deputy Assistant Secretary
   of State for Far Eastern Economic
   Affairs
Washington, D. C.

BERELSON, BERNARD
The Population Council
New York

BIRKELAND, Jorgen M.
Chairman
Department of Microbiology
Ohio State University

BOND, EDWARD L., JR.
President
Young & Rubicam, Inc.
New York

BROWNE, ROBERT S.
Phelps-Stokes Fund
New York

BUTLER, PIERCE, III
Doherty, Rumble & Butler
St. Paul

[1] In this connection attention is called to the recent report of the National Acad-
emy of Sciences—National Research Council on *Natural Resources.*

BUTTERFIELD, ALFRED
Chairman
United States Productions
New York

CABOT, HENRY B.
Boston

CHERNE, LEO
Executive Director
Research Institute of America
New York

CHILDERS, JAMES SAXON
President
Tupper & Love, Inc.
Atlanta

CHISHOLM, BROCK, M.D.
Victoria, British Columbia

COLIVER, MRS. NORMAN
The Asia Foundation
San Francisco

COOK, ROBERT C.
President
Population Reference Bureau
Washington, D. C.

CRONEIS, CAREY
Chancellor
William Marsh Rice University

DAVIS, HARTWELL, JR.
Harriman Scholar
Columbia University

DeVINNEY, LELAND C.
The Rockefeller Foundation
New York

DRAPER, WILLIAM H., JR.
Draper, Gaither & Anderson
Palo Alto

DUCOFF, LOUIS
Chief of Farm Population Branch
Economic Research Service
Department of Agriculture
Washington, D. C.

DUFFY, BENEDICT J., M.D.
Georgetown University School of
Medicine
Washington, D. C.

ECCLES, MARRINER S.
Chairman
First Security Corporation
Salt Lake City

FAGLEY, THE REV. RICHARD M.
Executive Secretary
Commission of the Churches on
International Affairs
New York

FAIN, JAMES E.
Editor
Dayton *Daily News*
Ohio

FINNEY, PAUL
Associate Managing Editor
Business Week
New York

FISHER, JOSEPH L.
President
Resources For The Future, Inc.
Washington, D. C.

FRIEDMAN, MARVIN
AFL-CIO Research Department
Washington, D. C.

GARDNER, RICHARD N.
Deputy Assistant Secretary of State for
International Organization Affairs
Washington, D. C.

GIVENS, MEREDITH B.
Director, Research Office in Economics
and Science
Department of State
Washington, D. C.

GORDIS, RABBI ROBERT
Temple Beth-El of Rockaway Park
New York

GREMILLION, THE RT. REV.
MONSIGNOR JOSEPH
Catholic Relief Services
New York

GUTTMACHER, ALAN F., M.D.
President
Planned Parenthood Association of
America
New York

HALSTED, HENRY, III
Associated Colleges of the Midwest
Chicago

HARKAVY, OSCAR
The Ford Foundation
New York

HAUSER, PHILIP M.
University of Chicago

HOVGARD, CARL
President
Research Institute of America, Inc.
New York

IMBIORSKI, THE REVEREND
WALTER J.
Cana Conference
Chicago

KAGAN, SIOMA
University of Oregon

KIRK, DUDLEY
The Population Council
New York

LEW, EDWARD A.
Vice President
Metropolitan Life Insurance Co.
New York

LIVINGSTON, GOODHUE
New York

LORIMER, FRANK W.
Department of Sociology
American University

McKELVEY, RAYMOND C.
Department of Political Science
Occidental College
Los Angeles

McNAMARA, ROBERT L.
Chairman
Department of Sociology
University of Missouri

MAREMONT, ARNOLD H.
President
Maremont Corporation
Chicago

MAY, MRS. CORDELIA SCAIFE
Ligonier, Pennsylvania

MOLYNEUX, ROBERT E.
Scripps-Howard Newspaper Alliance
Washington, D. C.

MOORE, HUGH
Chairman of the Board
Dixie Cup Company
Easton, Pennsylvania

MUDD, STUART, M.D.
U. S. Veterans Administration Hospital
Philadelphia

NOTESTEIN, FRANK W.
President
The Population Council
New York

NUVEEN, JOHN
John Nuveen & Co.
Chicago

OSBORN, FREDERICK
Chairman
The Population Council
New York

PICKERING, JAMES V.
President & Chairman
Esso Standard Eastern, Inc.
New York

PLIMPTON, FRANCIS T. P.
Deputy Representative of the
United States to the United Nations

PRICE, DAVID E., M.D.
Deputy Surgeon General
Washington, D. C.

REID, WHITELAW
Purchase, New York

REVELLE, ROGER
Dean of Research
The University of California
Berkeley

RIVLIN, MRS. ALICE
Brookings Institution
Washington, D. C.

ROSE, RABBI EMANUEL
Congregation Beth Israel
Portland, Oregon

ROSS, MICHAEL
Department of International Affairs
AFL-CIO
Washington, D. C.

SANSONE, ROBERT
Harriman Scholar
Columbia University

SCHLESINGER, THOMAS
Colonial Williamsburg
Virginia

SCHMIDT, ADOLPH W.
Vice President
T. Mellon & Sons
Pittsburgh

SEGAL, SHELDON
The Population Council
New York

SENIOR, CLARENCE
Department of Sociology
Brooklyn College

SHOEMAKER, DON
Editor
The Miami *Herald*
Florida

SMITH, FRANKLIN R., M.D.
Seattle

TAEUBER, CONRAD
Assistant Director
Bureau of the Census
Washington, D. C.

TAEUBER, MRS. CONRAD
Office of Population Research
Princeton University

TALMAGE, DAVID W., M.D.
University of Colorado Medical Center
Denver

THOMAS, THE REV. JOHN, S.J.
Institute of Social Order
St. Louis University

VAN NORT, LEIGHTON
Office of International Economic
   & Social Affairs
Department of State
Washington, D. C.

WEINLEIN, ANTHONY
Research Director
Building Service Employees
   International Union
Chicago

WHELPTON, P. K.
Director
Scripps Foundation for Population
   Research
Miami University, Ohio

WHITLOCK, FOSTER B.
President
Ortho Pharmaceutical Corp.
Raritan, New Jersey

WILLIAMSON, J. GASTON
Rose, Meek, House, Barron,
   Nash & Williamson
Little Rock

WILLISON, ROBERT E.
Laurel Foundation
Pittsburgh

YOUNG, DONALD
President
Russell Sage Foundation
New York

Since its establishment by Dwight D. Eisenhower at Columbia University in 1950, The American Assembly has held Assemblies of national leaders and has published books to illuminate issues of United States policy.

The Assembly is a national, nonpartisan educational institution, incorporated under the State of New York. It was the official administrator of the

President's Commission on National Goals, which reported to President Eisenhower late in 1960.

The Trustees of the Assembly approve a topic for presentation in a background book, authoritatively designed and written to aid deliberations at national Assembly sessions at Arden House. These books are also used to support discussion at regional Assembly sessions and to evoke consideration by the general public.

All sessions of the Assembly, whether international, national or local, issue and publicize independent reports of conclusions and recommendations on the topic at hand. Participants in these sessions constitute a wide range of experience and competence.

The American Assembly

A...   Series

ARMS CON...   , S-AA-4
AUTOMATI...   Dunlop, S-AA-7
THE CONC...   man, S-AA-13
CULTURAL...   Blum, S-AA-8
THE FEDE...   e, S-AA-14
GOALS FO...   MISSION ON NA-
  TIONAL...
OUTER SPA...
THE POPU...
THE SECR...
THE UNIT...   -AA-12
THE UNIT...   ited by Herbert
  L. Matt...
THE UNIT...   d by Willard L.
  Thorp,
THE UNIT...   iana G. Stevens,
  S-AA-11...

* Also available in clothbound edition.